Buddhism and the Bahá'í Faith

Buddhism

and

the Bahá'í Faith

An Introduction to the Bahá'í Faith
for Theravada Buddhists

by

MOOJAN MOMEN

GEORGE RONALD
OXFORD

GEORGE RONALD, Publisher
46 High Street, Kidlington, Oxford OX5 2DN

British Library Cataloguing in Publication Data

A catalogue record for this book is available
from the British Library

ISBN 0-85398-384-4 Pbk

Printed and bound in Great Britain by
Biddles Ltd, Guildford and King's Lynn

Contents

Introduction

This book is intended to be an introduction to the Bahá'í Faith for people who come from a Theravada Buddhist background. The Bahá'í Faith is the newest of the world religions. It was founded by Bahá'u'lláh over one hundred years ago and Bahá'ís are those who follow the teachings of Bahá'u'lláh. Bahá'ís believe that over the course of thousands of years there have been from time to time and in different parts of the world a small number of fully-enlightened ones. Their mission has been to guide humanity in its spiritual and social affairs. Bahá'ís believe that Bahá'u'lláh was the most recent of these teachers.

Although the Bahá'í Faith is only about 150 years old, in that short time it has spread to every corner of the planet. There are now Bahá'ís from every cultural and religious background in the world. Bahá'í communities exist in every country and they are all working towards the goals of a united humanity and world peace. Bahá'u'lláh has given teachings that will enable humankind to achieve these goals.

The Bahá'í Faith does not seek to undermine any religion. The Bahá'í scriptures acknowledge the station of Lord Buddha, and so everyone who becomes a Bahá'í must also come to believe in the Buddha. Nor does the Bahá'í Faith seek to impose any particular culture upon the world. The unity that it seeks to bring about is a unity in diversity. It teaches that now is the time for humanity to put aside all sources of conflict and strife, whether based on nationality, religion, race, class or caste, and to come together in unity.

This book will try to present the Bahá'í Faith in a way that explains its teaching to those from a background in Theravada Buddhism. Theravada Buddhism represents what is probably the oldest extant and largest grouping of Buddhists. Further, although the followers of the Theravada are found in a large area stretching from Sri Lanka, to Burma, Thailand and into Southeast Asia, there is a general agreement among them about the canon of scripture to which they adhere. It is for these reasons that it has been decided to concentrate on Theravada Buddhism in this short introductory work. Although there are also large number of Mahayana Buddhists, the various groupings of these do not hold a corpus of scripture and doctrines in common. If this book had tried to address all of these groups, it would have needed to be much larger than the brief introductory text that was intended. It will eventually, of course, be necessary for similar works to be written addressed to these other groupings of Buddhists.

The first chapter of the present book is intended to show that the ethical and moral teachings of the Bahá'í Faith and Buddhism are very similar. This confirms the statement by the Lord Buddha that the Path of *Dhamma* is eternal.

The second chapter deals with those areas that cause the most difficulties in reconciling different religious traditions. This is the area of metaphysics and includes questions such as the nature of Absolute Reality, the existence of a self and a soul, and what happens after death.

Chapter 3 deals with some of the prophecies in the Buddhist scriptures. Bahá'ís believe that Bahá'u'lláh is the fulfillment of the prophecies in the Buddhist scriptures that a further Buddha will come to the earth, the Metteyya Buddha.

In the fourth chapter there is a brief account of the life of

Bahá'u'lláh and of the world Bahá'í community at the present time.

However if, as asserted in Chapter 1, the Path of *Dhamma* is eternal, then why is there a need for a further Enlightened One to come and to bring a new message? Why do Bahá'ís not simply follow the Way of Buddha? The fifth chapter answers this question. It shows that although the Path of *Dhamma* is eternal, the practical way that its effect is channelled in human society changes and evolves. Thus the Buddha gave certain instructions for the organization of the *Sangha*. These instructions, although suitable for the time in which they were given, are no longer adequate to meet the requirements of the age in which we live. Hence the need for a new way of organizing the *Sangha*; for new social teachings that will bring humankind to unity and world peace.

Chapter 6 contains some details about the new laws given by Bahá'u'lláh for the new worldwide *Sangha* that he has inaugurated.

One of the cardinal teachings of both Bahá'u'lláh and Lord Buddha is that human beings must investigate reality for themselves: they must look into matters and discern the truth. For this reason the Bahá'í teachings and the Bahá'í scriptures have been translated into all of the most common languages of the world. This enables each person to investigate this new teaching for himself or herself, without having to rely on the interpretations and commentaries of others. Thus in Chapter 1, for example the Buddhist and Bahá'í scriptures have been translated and placed side by side so that each individual can judge for himself or herself the accuracy of the statement that the *Dhamma* taught by Bahá'u'lláh is not contradictory to the *Dhamma* of Lord Buddha.

Many Buddhist terms in this book are given in two forms: Pali followed by Sanskrit. This is because although the scriptures of Theravada Buddhism are written in Pali, many of the terms and concepts that they contain are more familiar in English in their Sanskrit form. A glossary of terms may be found after this Introduction.

Thanks are due to a number of people who have helped with this book. First and foremost is Katherine Chauhan (formerly Villiers-Stuart) whose manuscript 'The Bahá'í Message – Any Concern of Buddhists?' was one of the starting points of the present work. Others who have helped by commenting on the book as it has been developed are Mr Robert Parry, Dr Peter Smith of Mahidol University, Bangkok, and Mr M. L. C. Chandrasekera.

Glossary

In this glossary, the Pali term is given first followed by the Sanskrit where appropriate.

Anatta, anatman. The Buddhist doctrine that the idea of a self or an individual soul is a mistaken concept which causes attachment to the world and is an obstacle to realization of *nibbana.*

Anicca, anitya. The impermanence or transitoriness of the world and everything in it; everything is subject to change.

Arahat, Arhat. One who has progressed in the Path of *Dhamma* to the point where he will have no more rebirths and will acheive *nibbana.*

Aryan. Noble.

Avyakata, avyakrta. Hidden, indeterminable, inexpressible (those questions that the Buddha declared cannot be answered).

Bhikku, bhikshu. Monk, beggar.

Brahmin. A member of the Hindu priestly caste.

Dhamma, Dharma. The cosmic law which underlies our world and, in particular, the Buddha's teaching of this law.

Dukkha, Duhkha. The suffering which is an inherent part of this world.

Kamma, Karma. The universal law of cause and effect.

Khanda, Skandha (literally: aggregates). The elements that come together to form a being.

Maya. The illusion of reality which this world gives.

Nibbana, Nirvana (literally: extinction). The ultimate goal of Buddhist spiritual practice – an unconditioned state free of suffering and delusion.

Saddha. Faith or conviction.

Samsara. The phenomenal world, worldly existence, the cycles of existence.

Sangha. The Buddhist order or community of monks.

Tathagata (literally: the thus-gone one). A title of the Buddha, referring to one who has achieved supreme enlightenment.

Vinaya. The laws and regulations governing Buddhist monks.

Buddhism and the Bahá'í Faith

I

The Path – The *Dhamma*
Ethical and Moral Teachings

The Lord Buddha and Bahá'u'lláh both see humankind suffering. Their wish is to lead humanity out of its suffering. This they see as the most important part of their teaching – everything else is focused on this one point.

The Buddha says that the house of self is on fire, burning with hatred, lust and illusion. Humanity, he says, is like a man suffering from a poisoned arrow in his foot. He must urgently attend to the task of removing the arrow, which will otherwise destroy him. The Buddha is the physician, or doctor, who can pull the arrow out.[1]

Bahá'u'lláh uses a similar analogy regarding human beings. He says: 'So fierce is this fire of self burning within them, that at every moment they seem to be afflicted with fresh torments.'[2] He states that mankind is ill and is suffering: '. . . the whole human race is encompassed with great, with incalculable afflictions. We see it languishing on its bed of sickness, sore-tried and disillusioned.' But he, the healer, the divine physician 'perceiveth the disease, and prescribeth, in His unerring wisdom, the remedy.'[3]

The Lord Buddha, in his first sermon after his enlightenment, identifies both the problem and its cure. These are called the Four Noble Truths.

The First Noble Truth is that every part of our life (birth, old age, disease, death) is conditioned by change leading to suffering and sorrow:

This is the Noble Truth as to suffering: Birth is painful,

old age is painful, disease and death are painful; associa-
tion with what one dislikes is suffering; separation from
what one likes is suffering; not to get what one wants is
also suffering. In short, every part of us, because we grasp
hold of life, is subject to suffering.[4]

Similarly, in the Bahá'í writings, it is written:

Such is this mortal abode: a storehouse of afflictions and
suffering. It is ignorance that binds man to it, for no com-
fort can be secured by any soul in this world, from
monarch down to the most humble commoner. If once this
life should offer a man a sweet cup, a hundred bitter ones
will follow; such is the condition of this world.[5]

These brief few days shall pass away, this present life
shall vanish from our sight; the roses of this world shall be
fresh and fair no more, the garden of this earth's triumphs
and delights shall droop and fade. The spring season of life
shall turn into the autumn of death, the bright joy of
palace halls shall give way to moonless dark within the
tomb. And therefore is none of this worth loving at all, and
to this the wise will not anchor his heart.[6]

The Second Noble Truth taught by the Lord Buddha is that
the cause of this sorrow is our attachment to this world:

This is the Noble Truth about the origin of suffering: it is
ignorant craving which leads to rebirth. This is associated
with desire and attachment, the seeking of pleasure every-
where, the craving for happiness in this life or a future
one.[7]

Bahá'u'lláh sees the world in a similar way. The Bahá'í
teachings identify our attachment to the things of this
world as the cause of our sorrows.

If we suffer it is the outcome of material things, and all the
trials and troubles come from this world of illusion.
    For instance, a merchant may lose his trade and depres-
sion ensues. A workman is dismissed and starvation

stares him in the face. A farmer has a bad harvest, anxiety fills his mind. A man builds a house which is burnt to the ground and he is straightway homeless, ruined, and in despair.

All these examples are to show you that the trials which beset our every step, all our sorrow, pain, shame and grief, are born in the world of matter . . .[8]

Bahá'u'lláh likens humankind to a bird that has been attracted to the earth.

Could ye apprehend with what wonders of My munificence and bounty I have willed to entrust your souls, ye would, of a truth, rid yourselves of attachment to all created things, and would gain a true knowledge of your own selves . . . Suffer not your idle fancies, your evil passions, your insincerity and blindness of heart to dim the lustre, or stain the sanctity, of so lofty a station. Ye are even as the bird which soareth . . . through the immensity of the heavens, until, impelled to satisfy its hunger, it turneth longingly to the water and clay of the earth below it, and, having been entrapped in the mesh of its desire, findeth itself impotent to resume its flight to the realms whence it came. Powerless to shake off the burden weighing on its sullied wings, that bird, hitherto an inmate of the heavens, is now forced to seek a dwelling-place upon the dust. Wherefore . . . defile not your wings with the clay of waywardness and vain desires, and suffer them not to be stained with the dust of envy and hate, that ye may not be hindered from soaring in the heavens of My divine knowledge.[9]

The Third Noble Truth concerns the end of suffering. It is the putting an end to ignorant craving, giving up desire and attachment, abandoning pleasure-seeking and craving for life or for the cessation of life:[10]

Whoso in the world overcomes his selfish cravings, from him sorrows fall away, like water-drops from a lotus-leaf.[11]

3

Bahá'u'lláh also calls on people to detach themselves from the things of this world.

> Rejoice not in the things ye possess; tonight they are yours, tomorrow others will possess them.[12]

> O My Servant! Free thyself from the fetters of this world, and loose thy soul from the prison of self. Seize thy chance, for it will come to thee no more.[13]

> Disencumber yourselves of all attachment to this world and the vanities thereof. Beware that ye approach them not, inasmuch as they prompt you to walk after your own lusts and covetous desires, and hinder you from entering the straight and glorious Path.[14]

The Path (*Dhamma*) referred to in this last quotation was also mentioned by the Buddha as the Fourth Noble Truth. The Buddha calls this Path the Middle Way, the way of moderation that avoids extremes. By 'moderation' Lord Buddha was referring mainly to the avoidance of the extremes of excessive asceticism and extravagant indulgence. Bahá'u'lláh also praises the path of moderation and extends it to all matters.

> . . . the ninth leaf of the Most Exalted Paradise is this: In all matters moderation is desirable. If a thing is carried to excess, it will prove a source of evil.[15]

We human beings have only a short time upon the earth. All of the Buddhas have challenged us not to misuse this time but to seek out the Path and set out upon it. Gautama Buddha said:

> How can there be laughter, how can there be pleasure, when the whole world is burning? When you are in deep darkness, will you not ask for a lamp?[16]

> Yellow leaves hang on your tree of life. The messengers of death are waiting. You are going to travel far away. Have you any provision for the journey?[17]

4

Bahá'u'lláh, writing of the same situation, has said:

> Ages have passed and your precious lives are well-nigh ended, yet not a single breath of purity hath reached Our court of holiness from you.[18]

> I desire communion with thee, but thou wouldst put no trust in Me. The sword of thy rebellion hath felled the tree of thy hope. At all times I am near unto thee, but thou art ever far from Me. Imperishable glory I have chosen for thee, yet boundless shame thou hast chosen for thyself. While there is yet time, return, and lose not thy chance.[19]

This Path which we as human beings must follow if we are to escape from the suffering of this world is called by the Buddha the Eightfold Noble Path. As the Buddha described it, this path consists of:

1. Right View
2. Right Aim or Right-mindedness
3. Right Speech
4. Right Action
5. Right Living or Livelihood
6. Right Effort or Endeavour
7. Right Mindfulness
8. Right Contemplation

This sums up the fundamental ethical and moral teachings of the Buddha. Bahá'u'lláh's teachings uphold all eight of the elements of this path. To demonstrate this we will look at the Buddhist and Bahá'í scriptures side by side. In the following section all of the Buddhist quotations are taken from the well-known Buddhist scriptures in the Tripitaka. The Bahá'í quotations are taken from the Bahá'í scriptures.

The Eightfold Noble Path

Buddhist   Bahá'í

1. Right View

And what, bhikkus, is right view? The knowledge about ill, bhikkus, the knowledge about the coming to be of ill, knowledge about the way that leads to the cessation of ill. This is what is called right view.

Digha Nikaya[20]

The essence of all that We have revealed for thee is Justice, is for man to free himself from idle fancy and imitation, discern with the eye of oneness His glorious handiwork, and look into all things with a searching eye.

Bahá'u'lláh, Words of Wisdom[21]

He whose sight is illumined with the light of understanding will assuredly detach himself from the world and the vanities thereof . . . Let not the world and its vileness grieve you.

'Abdu'l-Bahá[22]

2. Right Aim

And what, bhikkus, is right aim? Being set on renunciation, on benevolence, on kindness. This is what is called right aim.

Digha Nikaya[23]

Universal benefits derive from the grace of the Divine religions, for they lead their true followers to sincerity of intent, to high purpose, to purity and spotless honour, to surpassing kindness and compassion, to the keeping of their covenants when they have covenanted, to concern for the rights of others, to liberality, to justice in every aspect of life, to humanity and philanthropy, to valour and to unflagging efforts in the service of mankind

'Abdu'l-Bahá, The Secret of Divine Civilization[24]

6

Buddhist   Bahá'í

3. Right Speech

And what, bhikkus, is right speech? Abstaining from lying, slander, abuse and idle talk. This is what is called right speech.
Digha Nikaya[25]

The gift of Truth excels all gifts. The taste of Truth excels all sweetness. The joy of Truth excels all pleasures.
Dhammapada[26]

Never speak harsh words, for once spoken they may return to you. Angry words are painful and there may be blows for blows.
Dhammapada[27]

A man whose words are lies, who transgresses the Great Law, and who scorns the higher world – there is no evil this man may not do.
Dhammapada[28]

A true seeker . . . must cling unto patience and resignation, observe silence, and refrain from idle talk. For the tongue is a smouldering fire, and excess of speech a deadly poison. Material fire consumeth the body, whereas the fire of the tongue devoureth both heart and soul. The force of the former lasteth but for a time, whilst the effects of the latter endure a century.

That seeker should also regard backbiting as grievous error, and keep himself aloof from its dominion, inasmuch as backbiting quencheth the light of the heart, and extinquisheth the life of the soul.
Bahá'u'lláh, Book of Certitude[29]

Truthfulness is the foundation of all the virtues of the world of humanity.
'Abdu'l-Bahá[30]

4. Right Action

And what, bhikkus, is right action? Abstaining from taking life, from taking what is not given, from carnal indulgence. This is what is called right action.
Digha Nikaya[31]

A man is not a follower of righteousness because he talks much learned talk; but although a man be not learned, if he forgets not the right path, if his work is rightly done, then he is a follower of righteousness.

Beware, O people of Bahá, lest ye walk in the ways of them whose words differ from their deeds . . . Let your acts be a guide unto all mankind, for the professions of most men, be they high or low, differ from their conduct. It is through your deeds that ye can distinguish yourselves from others . . . Happy is the man that heedeth My counsel.
Gleanings from the Writings of Bahá'u'lláh[32]

7

Buddhist

Better to do nothing than to do what is wrong, for wrongdoing brings burning sorrow. Do therefore what is right, for good deeds never bring pain.

Just as a flower which seems beautiful and has colour but has no perfume, so are the fruitless words of the man who speaks them and does them not.

Dhammapada[33]

Bahá'í

Guidance hath ever been given by words, and now it is given by deeds. Every one must show forth deeds that are pure and holy, for words are the property of all alike, whereas such deeds as these belong only to Our loved ones. Strive then with heart and soul to distinguish yourselves by your deeds. In this wise We counsel you in this holy and resplendent tablet.

The Hidden Words of Bahá'u'lláh[34]

The essence of faith is fewness of words and abundance of deeds; he whose words exceed his deeds, know verily that his death is better than his life.

Bahá'u'lláh, Words of Wisdom[35]

5. Right Living

And what, bhikkus, is right livelihood? Herein, bhikkus, the Aryan disciple puts away wrong livelihood and supports himself by right livelihood.

Digha Nikaya[36]

The best of men are they that earn a livelihood by their calling and spend upon themselves and upon their kindred . . .

The Hidden Words of Bahá'u'lláh[37]

It is enjoined upon every one of you to engage in some form of occupation, such as crafts, trades and the like . . . Waste not your time in idleness and sloth. Occupy yourselves with that which profiteth yourselves and others.

Glad-Tidings of Bahá'u'lláh[38]

8

Buddhist   Bahá'í

6. Right Effort

And what, bhikkus, is right effort? It is that a brother makes an effort that evil states that have not arisen in him, do not arise. To this end, he exerts himself, he applies his mind and struggles. Likewise he makes the same effort to put away the evil states that have already arisen within him. And likewise he does the same in order that the good states that have not arisen within him do arise. And likewise he does the same in order that good states that have arisen in him may become established, may not decay, may multiply and grow abundant, and come to perfection. This is what is called right effort.

Digha Nikaya[39]

Success or failure, gain or loss, must, therefore, depend upon man's own exertions. The more he striveth, the greater will be his progress.

Gleanings from the Writings of Bahá'u'lláh[40]

Arise, therefore, and, with the whole enthusiasm of your hearts, with all the eagerness of your souls, the full fervour of your will, and the concentrated efforts of your entire being, strive to attain the paradise of His presence . . . and to obtain a portion of this perfume of celestial glory.

Gleanings from the Writings of Bahá'u'lláh[41]

Our greatest efforts must be directed towards detachment from the things of the world; we must strive to become more spiritual, more luminous, to follow the counsel of the Divine Teaching, to serve the cause of unity and true equality . . .

'Abdu'l-Bahá, Paris Talks[42]

7. Right Mindfulness

And what, bhikkus, is right mindfulness? Herein, a brother continues to look upon the body in such a way that he remains ardent, self-possessed and mindful, having overcome both the covetousness and the dejection that is so common in the world. And similarly with regard to feel-

He is not to be numbered with the people of Bahá who followeth his mundane desires, or fixeth his heart on things of the earth. He is My true follower who, if he come to a valley of pure gold, will pass straight through it aloof as a cloud, and will neither turn back, nor pause. Such a man is,

Buddhist

ings, thoughts, ideas and activities; he looks upon these in such a way that he remains ardent, self-possessed and mindful, having overcome both the covetousness and the dejection that is so common in the world. This is what is called right mindfulness.

Digha Nikaya[43]

Bahá'í

assuredly, of Me . . . And if he met the fairest and most comely of women, he would not feel his heart seduced by the least shadow of desire for her beauty. Such an one, indeed, is the creation of spotless chastity.

Gleanings from the Writings of Bahá'u'lláh[44]

Live then the days of thy life, that are less than a fleeting moment, with thy mind stainless, thy heart unsullied, thy thoughts pure and thy nature sanctified, so that, free and content, thou mayest put away this mortal frame . . .

The Hidden Words of Bahá'u'lláh[45]

8. Right Contemplation

And what, bhikkus, is right contemplation? Herein, a brother aloof from sensuous appetites, remote from evil states, enters into and abides in the first stage of meditative contemplation, wherein there is cogitation and deliberation, which is born of solitude and full of joy and happiness. Suppressing cogitation and deliberation, he enters into and abides in the second stage of meditative contemplation, which is self-evoked, born of concentration, full of joy and happiness, in that, set free from cogitation and deliberation, the mind grows calm and sure, dwelling on high. And further, disenchanted with joy, he abides calmly contemplative while, mindful and self-possessed, he feels in his body that happiness

. . . while you meditate you are speaking with your own spirit. In that state of mind you put certain questions to your spirit and the spirit answers: the light breaks forth and the reality is revealed . . .

The spirit of man is itself informed and strengthened during meditation; through it affairs of which man knew nothing are unfolded before his view . . .

Meditation is the key for opening the doors of mysteries. In that state man abstracts himself; in that state man withdraws himself from all outside objects; in that subjective mood he is immersed in the ocean of spiritual life and can unfold the secrets of things-in-themselves. To illustrate this, think of man as endowed with two

Buddhist

whereof Aryans declare: 'He that is calmly contemplative and aware, he dwells in happiness.' So does he enter into and dwell in the third stage of meditative contemplation. And further, by putting aside happiness and malaise, by the passing away of joy and of melancholy, he enters into the fourth stage of meditative contemplation, where he is in a state of perfect purity of mindfulness and equanimity, wherein there is felt neither pain nor pleasure.

Digha Nikaya[46]

Bahá'í

kinds of sight; when the power of insight is being used the outward power of vision does not see.

This faculty of meditation frees man from the animal nature, discerns the reality of things . . .

The meditative faculty is akin to the mirror: if you put it before earthly objects it will reflect them. Therefore if the spirit of man is contemplating earthly subjects he will be informed of these.

But if you turn the mirror of your spirits heavenwards, the heavenly constellations and the rays of the Sun of Reality will be reflected in your hearts, and the virtues of the Kingdom will be obtained.

'Abdu'l-Bahá, Paris Talks[47]

There are also many other areas in which the Buddha's teachings and those of Bahá'u'lláh are very similar. The following are a few further examples:

Buddhist

Bahá'í

Death overshadows us all

Death carries away the man who gathers the flowers of sensuous passions, even as a torrent of rushing waters overflows a sleeping village, and then runs forward on its way.

Dhammapada[48]

O Children of Negligence! Set not your affections on mortal sovereignty and rejoice not therein. Ye are even as the unwary bird that with full confidence warbleth upon the bough; till of a sudden the fowler Death throws it upon the dust, and the melody, the form and the colour are gone, leaving not a trace. Wherefore take heed, O bondslaves of desire!

The Hidden Words of Bahá'u'lláh[49]

Buddhist   Bahá'í

Look not at the sins of others

Think not the faults of others, of what they have done or not done. Think rather of your own sins, of the things you have done or not done.

It is easy to see the faults of others, but difficult to see one's own faults. One shows the faults of others like chaff winnowed in the wind, but one conceals one's own faults as a cunning gambler conceals his dice. If a man sees the sins of others and for ever thinks of their faults, his own sins increase for ever and far off is he from the end of his faults.

Dhammapada[50]

How couldst thou forget thine own faults and busy thyself with the faults of others?

Breathe not the sins of others so long as thou art thyself a sinner.

If the fire of self overcome you, remember your own faults and not the faults of My creatures, inasmuch as every one of you knoweth his own self better than he knoweth others.

Speak no evil, that thou mayest not hear it spoken unto thee, and magnify not the faults of others that thine own faults may not appear great . . .

The Hidden Words of Bahá'u'lláh[51]

Avoid companionship of evil men

Have not for friends those whose soul is ugly; go not with men who have an evil soul. Have for friends those whose soul is beautiful; go with men whose soul is good.

Dhammapada[52]

O My Son! The company of the ungodly increaseth sorrow, whilst fellowship with the righteous cleanseth the rust from off the heart.

The Hidden Words of Bahá'u'lláh[53]

Kindness to animals

He who hurts not any creatures, whether feeble or strong, who neither kills nor causes to kill – him I call a Brahmin.

Dhammapada[54]

But to blessed animals the utmost kindness must be shown, the more the better.

'Abdu'l-Bahá[55]

Buddhist

Bahá'í

Joy

O let us live in joy, in love amongst those who hate! Among men who hate, let us live in love.

O let us live in joy, although having nothing! In joy let us live like spirits of light.

Dhammapada[56]

Joy gives us wings! In times of joy our strength is more vital, our intellect keener, and our understanding less clouded.

'Abdu'l-Bahá, Paris Talks[57]

Contentment

Contentment is the greatest treasure.

Dhammapada[58]

Content thyself with but little of this world's goods!

'Abdu'l-Bahá[59]

Non-injury and non-violence

All beings tremble before danger, all fear death. When a man considers this, he does not kill or cause to kill.

He who for the sake of happiness hurts others who also want happiness, shall not hereafter be happy.

He who for the sake of happiness does not hurt others who also want happiness, shall hereafter find happiness.

He who hurts with his weapons those who are harmless and pure shall soon fall into one of ten evils . . .

Dhammapada[60]

In every instance let the friends be considerate and infinitely kind. Let them never be defeated by the malice of the people, by their aggression and their hate, no matter how intense. If others hurl their darts against you, offer them milk and honey in return; if they poison your lives, sweeten their souls; if they injure you, teach them how to be comforted; if they inflict a wound upon you, be a balm to their sores; if they sting you, hold to their lips a refreshing cup.

'Abdu'l-Bahá[61]

Forbearance

Forbearing Patience is the highest devotion.

Dhammapada[62]

Show forbearance and benevolence and love to one another.

Gleanings from the Writings of Bahá'u'lláh[63]

Buddhist	Bahá'í

Purity

If a man speaks or acts with a pure mind, happiness follows him, even as his own shadow.
Dhammapada[64]

We verily behold your actions. If We perceive from them the sweet smelling savour of purity and holiness, We will most certainly bless you.
Gleanings from the Writings of Bahá'u'lláh[65]

Love

Hate is not conquered by hate; hate is conquered by love. This is an eternal law.
Dhammapada[66]

Know thou . . . that in every age and dispensation all Divine Ordinances are changed and transformed according to the requirements of the time, except the law of love, which, like unto a fountain, flows always and is never overtaken by change.
Bahá'u'lláh[67]

In the world of existence there is indeed no greater power than the power of love.
'Abdu'l-Bahá, Paris Talks[68]

Generosity

Misers go not to the celestial realms, and fools do not praise liberality; the wise man rejoices in giving, and thereby becomes happy in the realms above.
Dhammapada[69]

To give and to be generous are attributes of Mine; well is it with him that adornest himself with My virtues.
Hidden Words of Bahá'u'lláh[70]

Conquering anger

Forsake anger, give up pride.

Conquer anger by love; conquer evil by good.
Dhammapada[71]

Let nothing grieve thee, and be thou angered at none.
'Abdu'l-Bahá[72]

A thought of hatred must be destroyed by a more powerful thought of love.
'Abdu'l-Bahá, Paris Talks[73]

Buddhist   Bahá'í

Summary of Virtue

So long as the brethren shall persevere in kindness of action, speech, and thought amongst the saints, both in public and in private – so long as they shall divide without partiality, and share in common with the upright and the holy, all such things as they receive in accordance with the just provisions of the order, down even to the mere contents of a begging bowl – so long as the brethren shall live among the saints in the practice, both in public and in private, of those virtues which (unbroken, intact, unspotted, unblemished) are productive of freedom, and praised by the wise; which are untarnished by the desire of future life, or by the belief in the efficacy of outward acts; and which are conducive to high and holy thoughts – so long as the brethren shall live among the saints, cherishing, both in public and in private, that noble and saving faith which leads to the complete destruction of the sorrow of him who acts according to it — so long may the brethren be expected not to decline, but to prosper.

Maha-Parinibbana-Sutta[74]

Be generous in prosperity, and thankful in adversity. Be worthy of the trust of thy neighbour, and look upon him with a bright and friendly face. Be a treasure to the poor, an admonisher to the rich, an answerer of the cry of the needy, a preserver of the sanctity of thy pledge. Be fair in thy judgement, and guarded in thy speech. Be unjust to no man, and show all meekness to all men. Be as a lamp unto them that walk in darkness, a joy to the sorrowful, a sea for the thirsty, a haven for the distressed, an upholder and defender of the victim of oppression. Let integrity and uprightness distinguish all thine acts. Be a home for the stranger, a balm to the suffering, a tower of strength for the fugitive. Be eyes to the blind, and a guiding light unto the feet of the erring. Be an ornament to the countenance of truth, a crown to the brow of fidelity, a pillar of the temple of righteousness, a breath of life to the body of mankind, an ensign of the hosts of justice, a luminary above the horizon of virtue, a dew to the soil of the human heart, an ark on the ocean of knowledge, a sun in the heaven of bounty, a gem on the diadem of wisdom, a shining light in the firmament of thy generation, a fruit upon the tree of humility.

Gleanings from the Writings of Bahá'u'lláh[75]

15

Merit-Making

One of the main religious activities carried out by Buddhists in every country is merit-making, the performance of religious acts in order to gain religious merit. Bahá'u'lláh has also taught many ways of making merit. The main way is through living our lives according to his teachings and laws. We can also make merit by prayer and fasting (see Chapter 6); undertaking our daily work in the spirit of service; educating ourselves and educating children; giving to the Bahá'í funds; and by spreading the teachings of Bahá'u'lláh to those whom we meet.

The Structure of Existence
Metaphysical Teachings

One important area of religious teaching concerns such matters as the nature of the self or soul, the nature of the Absolute or God, and the question of salvation and what occurs after death. This is the area that is often the cause of the greatest differences among religions. When the Buddha was asked about such matters, he refused to be drawn into theorizing about them. No statements about such questions can adequately convey the reality. Therefore the Buddha discouraged his followers from concentrating on these things and relegated them to the realm of the *avyakatas*, the indeterminables (see below).

On one occasion, Malunkyaputta asked the Buddha several questions: whether the world is eternal or not, whether the world is finite or infinite, whether the soul and the body are identical or not, and about the existence of the saint after death. He received no reply but instead the Buddha related a parable:

It is as if a man is hit by a poison arrow. His friends hasten to the doctor. The latter is about to draw the arrow out of the wound. The wounded man however cries: 'Stop, I will not have the arrow drawn out until I know who shot it. Whether a warrior or a Brahmin, or belonging to the agricultural or menial castes . . . his name and to which family he belonged . . . whether he was tall or short . . . of what species and description the arrow was.'[1]

In seeking to obtain absolute knowledge of all of the circumstances of the shooting, the man had neglected the practical matter of removing the arrow and would certainly die. Similarly, the Buddha asserts that were he to try to elucidate the answers to the questions put to him by Malunkyaputta, 'that person would die before the Tathagata [a title of the Buddha] had ever elucidated this to him'.[2]

To each of the questions that the Buddha considered among those things that cannot be determined, Bahá'u'lláh provides a little more explanation but basically a similar answer. As to the question of whether the world is eternal or not, Bahá'u'lláh's answer is much the same as the Buddha's:

> As regards thine assertions about the beginning of creation, this is a matter on which conceptions vary by reason of the divergences in men's thoughts and opinions. Wert thou to assert that it hath ever existed and shall continue to exist, it would be true; or wert thou to affirm the same concept as is mentioned in the sacred Scriptures [i.e. that the world had a beginning and will have an end], no doubt would there be about it . . .[3]

To the second question of Malunkyaputta – whether the world is infinite or not – Bahá'u'lláh again asserts that the truth of this matter is difficult to explain because it is a relative truth.

> As to thy question whether the physical world is subject to any limitations, know thou that the comprehension of this matter dependeth upon the observer himself. In one sense, it is limited; in another, it is exalted beyond all limitations.[4]

Regarding the question of the nature of the self or soul, Bahá'u'lláh writes that it is a sign 'whose reality the most learned of men hath failed to grasp, and whose mystery no mind, however acute, can ever hope to unravel'.[5]

Linking this issue with the unknowability of Absolute Reality, Bahá'u'lláh states:

> Wert thou to ponder in thine heart, from now until the end that hath no end, and with all the concentrated intelligence and understanding which the greatest minds have attained in the past or will attain in the future, this divinely ordained and subtle Reality [the rational soul] . . . *thou wilt fail to comprehend its mystery . . . Having recognized thy powerlessness to attain to an adequate understanding of that Reality which abideth within thee,* thou wilt readily admit the futility of such efforts as may be attempted by thee, or by any of the created things, to fathom the mystery of the Living God . . . This confession of helplessness which mature contemplation must eventually impel every mind to make is in itself the acme of human understanding, and marketh the culmination of man's development.[6] (emphasis added)

Although Bahá'u'lláh uses terms – such as 'God' – derived from Judaeo-Christian-Islamic theology, in fact, he, like the Buddha, discourages his followers from spending too much time trying to understand these matters for, he states, they will never be understood in any absolute sense. About an understanding of the Absolute, God, Bahá'u'lláh writes:

> Every attempt to attain to an understanding of His inaccessible Reality hath ended in complete bewilderment, and every effort to approach His exalted Self and envisage His Essence hath resulted in hopelessness and failure.[7]

Bahá'u'lláh in his writings uses the term 'God' whereas the Buddha uses such expressions as the 'Unborn, Unoriginated' (see below, The Absolute). But both are agreed that these are merely words used as a label for something which the human mind can never comprehend. Thus all descriptions and attempts to explain this reality are true only in a relative sense and it is possible even for contradictory statements to be true. When we are dealing with matters relating to the 'Unborn, Unoriginated, Uncreated, Unformed', each culture and tradition has a different way of viewing these things and their statements about them may appear to be different. These differences, however, are due to the limitations of this world (*Samsara*). The reality is one and is transcendent to our feeble attempts to portray it.

Having established that absolute knowledge of such matters is impossible to attain, the Bahá'í position is that the different understandings of these matters in the different religious systems of the world are all aspects of the truth. Each religious system gives its own understanding from its own viewpoint. Each understanding is correct within its own perspective, even though it may appear to be radically different from others.[8] Therefore, since the Bahá'í Faith considers the metaphysical systems of every established religion to be valid representations of the truth, it is not surprising to find in the Bahá'í scriptures passages that are parallel to Buddhist metaphysical conceptions. These Bahá'í concepts are often couched in terms that are alien to Buddhism – the terminology of Judaeo-Christian-Islamic theology, which was, after all, the only language available to Bahá'u'lláh in which he could communicate with those around him. These terms are only the result of the limitations of *Samsara* (worldly existence) in trying to describe the Absolute. If one looks beyond the terms themselves to the image that they are conveying, one can find strong correspondences between Bahá'í and Buddhist concepts.

As examples of the correspondences between the Bahá'í Faith and Buddhism, we will here consider several doctrinal areas: the nature of this world (*Anicca* and *Maya*), the Absolute, the nature of Buddhahood, *Anatta* (no self) and Rebirth. For each of these concepts there are passages in the writings of Bahá'u'lláh that convey similar ideas.

The Impermanence of this World (*Anicca*)

Everything that is part of this world changes. Whatever has come into existence must over the course of time change and eventually cease to exist. The Buddha states:

> How transient are all component things!
> Growth is their nature and decay:
> They are produced, they are dissolved again.[9]

Bahá'u'lláh also frequently refers to the 'fleeting' nature of this world. He states that even if the world were to be enduring,

> . . . to set their affections upon it would still be unseemly for such as have quaffed, from the hands of Thy mercy, the wine of Thy presence; how much more when they recognize its fleetingness and are persuaded of its transience. The chances that overtake it, and the changes to which all things pertaining unto it are continually subjected, attest its impermanence.[10]

> Fleeting are the riches of the world; all that perisheth and changeth is not, and hath never been, worthy of attention, except to a recognized measure.[11]

Bahá'u'lláh relates that when he was a child at the wedding of one of his brothers, he watched a puppet show. The story of the puppet show was set in a palace and there were several puppets depicting the members of the royal court. When it ended, however, Bahá'u'lláh watched as the puppeteers packed all the finely-clothed figures into a trunk. Bahá'u'lláh saw this as a metaphor for the illusory and ephemeral trappings of the world and all earthly glory.

The Illusory Nature of this World (*Maya*)

This world impresses itself upon us as reality. But its reality is only an illusion. The Buddha teaches that:

When a man considers this world as a bubble of froth, and as the illusion of an appearance, then the king of death has no power over him.[12]

Similar to the Buddhist teaching of *Maya* is Bahá'u'lláh's teaching that:

The world is but a show, vain and empty, a mere nothing, bearing the semblance of reality. Set not your affections upon it . . . Verily I say, the world is like the vapour in a desert, which the thirsty dreameth to be water and striveth after it with all his might, until when he cometh unto it, he findeth it to be mere illusion.[13]

Elsewhere in the Bahá'í scriptures we find this world referred to as a 'mirage':

This present life is even as a swelling wave, or a mirage, or drifting shadows. Could ever a distorted image on the desert serve as refreshing waters? No, by the Lord of Lords! Never can reality and the mere semblance of reality be one, and wide is the difference between fancy and fact, between truth and the phantom thereof.

Know thou that the Kingdom is the real world, and this nether place is only its shadow stretching out. A shadow hath no life of its own; its existence is only a fantasy, and nothing more; it is but images reflected in water, and seeming as pictures to the eye.[14]

Since the world is ever-changing, impermanent and illusory, we are instructed by the Buddhas to give no importance to it. Gautama Buddha states:

See, Ananda, how all these things are now past, are ended, have vanished away. Thus impermanent, Ananda, are component things; thus transitory, Ananda, are component things; thus untrustworthy are component things. Insomuch, Ananda, is it meet to be weary of, is it meet to be estranged from, is it meet to be set quite free from the bondage of all component things![15]

Bahá'u'lláh has written:

> Abandon not the everlasting beauty for a beauty that must die, and set not your affections on this mortal world of dust.[16]

The Absolute

Fortunately, the Buddhas have assured us that behind this impermanent world and its illusions there is a reality, the Absolute Reality; and because of this it is possible for us to escape from the sorrow caused by the chances and changes of this world.

Gautama Buddha speaks of the Supramundane (*Lokuttara, Lokottara*) or Unconditioned (*Asankhata, Asamskrta*). This being beyond our world, we have no adequate words to speak of the Absolute. The following is the Buddha's description of it in the famous verse in the Udana passage in the *Khuddaka Nikaya*:

> There is, O monks, an Unborn, Unoriginated, Uncreated, Unformed. Were there not, O monks, this Unborn, Unoriginated, Uncreated, Unformed, there would be no escape from the world of the born, originated, created, formed. Since, O monks, there is an Unborn, Unoriginated, Uncreated, Unformed, therefore is there an escape from the born, originated, created, formed. What is dependant, that also moves; what is independent does not move. Where there is no movement, there is rest; where rest is, there is no desire; where there is no desire, there is neither coming nor going, no ceasing-to-be, no further coming to be. Where there is no ceasing-to-be, no further coming-to-be, there is neither this shore (this world) nor the other shore (*Nibbana*), nor anything between them.[17]

Bahá'u'lláh similarly speaks of an entity, an Unknowable Essence, of which nothing can be predicated:

> To every discerning and illumined heart it is evident that

God, the unknowable Essence, the divine Being, is immensely exalted beyond every human attribute, such as corporeal existence, ascent and descent, egress and regress . . . He standeth exalted beyond and above all separation and union, all proximity and remoteness. No sign can indicate His presence or His absence . . . [18]

Bahá'u'lláh is not here referring to a personified God as many consider God to be. Although the Buddha speaks of the 'Unborn, Unoriginated' and Bahá'u'lláh speaks of 'God', it is clear from the above quotations that they are referring to the same entity, an entity which is beyond human knowledge and understanding.

Buddhist teaching describes the world, *Samsara*, as the realm of impermanence, constant change and ceaseless becoming. It appears to be real but this reality is merely an illusion, *Maya*; only the Absolute truly exists and is real. *Samsara* exists and has reality only relative to the Absolute – it can have no independent, separate reality, for were *Samsara* to have any independent reality, the Absolute Reality would cease to be Absolute.

Bahá'u'lláh also considers this phenomenal world to be a relative reality only, while absolute reality applies to God alone:

'Absolute existence is strictly confined to God . . .'[19]

The Soul or Self

As we have seen above, the Buddha regards the existence of the self or soul as one of those matters that cannot be determined. Any statement about it – even to say either that it exists or does not exist – is to take a dogmatic position and this does not accord with the reality of the situation. We have also seen that Bahá'u'lláh too regards any statements or conceptualizations about the self or soul as being far from the truth (see pp. 18–19).

The soul or self is regarded as a relative or contingent existence in the writings of Bahá'u'lláh. After death:

> . . . it will assume the form that best befitteth its immortality and is worthy of its celestial habitation. Such an existence is a contingent and not an absolute existence . . .[20]

> For the mere mention of any one of Thy creatures would in itself imply an assertion of their existence before the court of Thy singleness and unity. Such an assertion would be naught but open blasphemy, an act of impiety, the essence of profanity and a wanton crime. [21]

These two quotations are already tending towards the Buddhist concept of *Anatta* (no self). The Bahá'í writings are full of statements about the nothingness of self. For example, in writing of one aspect of the station of Buddhahood, Bahá'u'lláh states that they (the Buddhas of every age), when comparing themselves to the Absolute,

> . . . have considered themselves as utterly effaced and non-existent . . . they have regarded themselves as utter nothingness, and deemed their mention in that Court an act of blasphemy. For the slightest whisperings of self, within such a Court, is an evidence of self-assertion and independent existence. In the eyes of them who have attained unto that Court, such a suggestion is itself a grievous transgression.[22]

In considering the stages of the human being's journey to the ultimate goal, Bahá'u'lláh names the last of these stages 'the Valley of True Poverty and Absolute Nothingness'. Put into Buddhist terms, this passage states that in order for human beings to achieve their ultimate goal of the Absolute, they must die to their selves and extinguish all attachments to this world of *Samsara*.[23]

Thus both Lord Buddha and Bahá'u'lláh feel unable to make any dogmatic statements about the self or soul because such statements can never convey the truth. Reality is transcendent to thought and conceptualizations. But just as the Buddha turns people's attention away from dogma to the practical matter of the individual's spiritual progress through suppressing the fire of craving and desire generated by the self, the human ego, so also Bahá'u'lláh emphasizes the need for human beings to liberate themselves from the 'bondage of self'.[24]

> Arise, O people, and . . . resolve to gain the victory over your own selves, that haply the whole earth may be freed and sanctified from its servitude to the gods of its idle fancies − gods that have inflicted such loss upon, and are responsible for the misery of, their wretched worshippers. These idols form the obstacle that impedeth man in his efforts to advance in the path of perfection.[25]

Rebirth and *Kamma* (*Karma*)

Lord Buddha came to a society that was already steeped in Hindu ideas and concepts. One of the most important of these was the concept of rebirth. The Buddha reinterpreted this. Since Buddhism teaches the concept of *Anatta* (no self), it is not the self of a person that returns but the collection of the five *khandas* (*skandhas*) − the predispositions and characteristics of an individual − that does so. This concept is similar to the Bahá'í teaching that in every age there occurs the return of certain individuals from previous ages − not in the sense that there is a return of the self-same person, but that there is the return of the personality characteristics of such a person.

This is most clearly shown in the life-histories of the Buddhas themselves. Thus, for example, whenever a Buddha, a supremely enlightened One, arises, there are certain personality types who immediately respond and become his disciples while others oppose him and try to limit his influence and even harm him. These personality types, these collections of particular *khandas*, are called in the Bahá'í writings the 'returns' of those people of a previous age. Thus we are told in the *Jataka Tales* that in former ages, in the previous births of Gautama Buddha, Devadatta had tried to harm him then also.[26] And so, for example, Mírzá Yaḥyá, who opposed and betrayed Bahá'u'lláh, can be regarded as the return of Judas Iscariot, who was a disciple of Jesus Christ and betrayed him. Judas can in turn be regarded as a return of Devadatta, who betrayed the Buddha. Similarly, the companions of Bahá'u'lláh who accompanied him in the stages of his exiles can be regarded as the return of the twelve disciples of Christ who in turn are the return of the those monks who gathered around Gautama Buddha.

The Buddhist concept of rebirth is strongly linked to the Law of *Kamma* – cause and effect. Thus the suffering that happens to us is the direct result of deeds that we have committed in the past.

In the Bahá'í scriptures there is also the concept of cause and effect:

> The trials of man are of two kinds. (a) The consequences of his own actions. If a man eats too much, he ruins his digestion; if he takes poison he becomes ill or dies. If a man gambles he will lose money . . .[27]

However, this law of cause and effect is only one of the reasons that suffering afflicts human beings. The same passage goes on to give a second reason for trials and suffering:

> (b) Other sufferings there are, which come upon the Faithful . . . Those who suffer most, attain to the greatest perfection.
>
> . . . Grief and sorrow do not come to us by chance, they are sent to us by the Divine Mercy for our own perfecting.
>
> . . . Men who suffer not, attain no perfection. The plant

most pruned by the gardeners is that one which, when the summer comes, will have the most beautiful blossoms and the most abundant fruit.

The labourer cuts up the earth with his plough, and from that earth comes the rich and plentiful harvest. The more a man is chastened, the greater is the harvest of spiritual virtues shown forth by him. A soldier is no good General until he has been in the front of the fiercest battle and has received the deepest wounds.[28]

Therefore it is the Bahá'í belief that the whole of our lives on this earth is a process of perfecting and spiritualizing ourselves, detaching ourselves from the excesses of the material world. The difficulties and tests that come to us can help us to do this if we approach them in the right way.

The usual Buddhist view is that after death one returns to this world, or rather, the collection of *khandas* that we are returns. Bahá'ís believe that there are many worlds or planes of existence beyond this one, through which we progress after death. The distinction is that between a circle, where one keeps coming back to the same place, and a spiral, where one keeps moving upwards and making progress towards the Absolute. Although this does represent a difference, the essential point is that both Buddhism and the Bahá'í Faith are agreed that our efforts and our actions in this world have an effect on this progress.

An analogy is found in the Bahá'í writings between our life in this world as a preparation for what comes after death, and the life of the embryo in the womb of its mother, preparing itself for this world.

For just as the effects and the fruitage of the uterine life are not to be found in that dark and narrow place, and only when the child is transferred to this wide earth do the benefits and uses of growth and development in that previous world become revealed – so likewise reward and punishment, heaven and hell, requital and retribution for actions done in this present life, will stand revealed in that other world beyond. And just as, if human life in the womb were limited to that uterine world, existence there would be nonsensical, irrelevant – so too if the life of this world, the deeds here done and their fruitage, did not come forth in the world beyond, the whole process would be irrational and foolish. [29]

Nibbana (Nirvana)

European commentators over the years have tended to suggest that the Buddha's teachings were nihilistic. This view particularly arose in connection with the scriptures describing *Nibbana*. Both Buddhists and Bahá'ís would agree that although *Nibbana* involves cessation, this does not refer to annihilation. It refers to the cessation of ignorance, of sorrow, and of cravings. As with other metaphysical concepts, Lord Buddha found no words that could adequately describe the state of *Nibbana*.

No measure measures him who enters rest. There is no word with which to speak of him. All thought is here at an end and so therefore all paths that words can take are also closed.[30]

Bahá'u'lláh also agrees that there is no adequate description of this state:

The movement of My Pen is stilled when it attempteth to befittingly describe the loftiness and glory of so exalted a station.[31]

Because there is no positive way to describe the person who has attained *Nibbana*, Lord Buddha mainly uses negative descriptions of this state.

There is, O monks, a state where there is neither earth nor water, nor heat, nor air; not infinity of space nor infinity of consciousness, nor nothingness; neither perception nor non-perception; neither this world nor that world; neither sun nor moon. That, O monks, I term neither coming nor going, nor standing; neither death nor birth. It is without stability, without change; it is without support, without beginning, without foundations; just that is the end of sorrows.[32]

The Buddha asserts that *Nibbana* is a state in which all desires and cravings have been destroyed[33] and in which there is complete control of the senses.[34] But above all, *Nibbana* is the state in which the ego is extinguished: 'The "I am" conceit is rooted out.'[35]

It is clear from the statements of the Buddha that this state is one which is achievable 'here and now', during this lifetime.

Those whose mind is well trained in the path of enlightenment, who cling not to anything and find joy in this freedom from attachment, whose passions have been overcome and who shine with a pure light, these shall attain Nibbana even in this mortal life.[36]

If one can attain *Nibbana* while still alive in this world, it is clear that this is not annihilation: it is a state to which human beings can aspire during this life.

Bahá'u'lláh also urges us to be free from attachments, so we can enter this liberated state:

Cast away that which ye possess, and, on the wings of detachment, soar beyond all created things.[37]

Pass beyond the narrow retreats of your evil and corrupt desires . . . and abide ye in the meads of sanctity and of detachment . . .[38]

Cleanse thyself from the defilement of riches and in perfect peace advance into the realm of poverty; that from the well-spring of detachment thou mayest quaff the wine of immortal life.[39]

Indeed the purpose of all of the great founders of the world's religions has been 'to educate all men, that they may, at the hour of death, ascend, in the utmost purity and sanctity and with absolute detachment, to the throne of the Most High'.[40]

And if we succeed, Bahá'u'lláh's description of the goal of our endeavour echoes the Buddhist descriptions of *Nibbana*:

> O Son of Worldliness! Pleasant is the realm of being, wert thou to attain thereto; glorious is the domain of eternity, shouldst thou pass beyond the world of mortality; sweet is the holy ecstasy if thou drinkest of the mystic chalice from the hands of the celestial Youth. Shouldst thou attain this station, thou wouldst be freed from destruction and death, from toil and sin.[41]

If we achieve this state of detachment, this state of the cessation of craving, we have entered the spiritual kingdom (*Nibbana*) in which suffering (*dukkha*) does not affect us:

> . . . the spiritual Kingdom never causes sadness. A man living with his thoughts in this Kingdom knows perpetual joy. The ills all flesh is heir to do not pass him by, but they only touch the surface of his life, the depths are calm and serene.[42]

The *Avyakatas*, the Indeterminables

In discussing and describing all of these points in the teachings of Gautama Buddha and Bahá'u'lláh, we must never lose sight of what was mentioned at the beginning of this chapter: that these questions about the structure of being and about ultimate reality cannot, in the end, be determined (*avyakata, avyakrtavastuni*). We may investigate and contemplate them but we will never fully understand them because the total truth about them is inexpressible. We can only understand aspects of this truth. This, the Bahá'í teachings state, is the reason for the differences among religions about these questions. The different religions disagree over these questions because they are each looking at differing aspects of these truths.

Further, we must not forget the Buddha's instructions that too much consideration of these questions is harmful because it distracts us from the important matter of how to attain enlightenment. One day, it is recorded, Vacchagatta the Wanderer asked about the Self and the Buddha made no reply. Later when he was asked by his chief disciple, Ananda, concerning his silence, the Buddha replied:

> If, Ananda, when asked by the Wanderer: 'Is there a self?' I had replied to him: 'There is a self', then, Ananda, that would have been siding with the recluses and Brahmins who are eternalists. But if, Ananda, when asked: 'Is there not a self?' I had replied that it does not exist, that, Ananda, would be siding with those recluses and Brahmins who are annihilationists.[43]

In other words, if Lord Buddha had answered the question, he would have been forced to side with one theory or another. But the Buddha considered that the real answer lay beyond all theories and concepts, therefore he was unable to answer the question without confusing the listener. Also, such questions distract the individual from the important and urgent task of salvation, which in no way depends on an understanding of these matters.

> To hold that the world is eternal or to hold that it is not, to agree to any other of the propositions that you adduce, Vaccha, is the jungle of theorizing, the tangle of theorizing, the bondage and the shackles of theorizing; it is coupled with misery, ruin, despair and agony; it conduces not to detachment, passionlessness, tranquillity, peace, to knowledge and wisdom of Nibbana. This is the danger I perceive in these views which makes me discard them all.[44]

And so the Buddha refused to be drawn into theorizing on these and other metaphysical questions. He discouraged his followers from concentrating on such matters. The Buddha relegated metaphysical questions to the realm of the *avyakatas*, the those questions that cannot be answered. When the Buddha was asked such questions, he usually maintained silence.

Bahá'u'lláh basically agrees with the Buddha that these metaphysical questions cannot be answered by a statement; for an answer assumes that it is possible to comprehend these matters, whereas in fact no absolute conceptual knowledge of them can be gained by the finite mind of humans.

Thus if we do discern any differences between the Buddhist position and the Bahá'í on any of the issues dealt with in this chapter, let us bear in mind that both views may be right – each from its own perspective. More importantly, let us bear in mind that both Gautama Buddha and Bahá'u'lláh emphasized that we should not become distracted by such matters. We should concentrate our attention on the practical question of how we attain to enlightenment. We should, then, turn our thoughts away from the contents of this chapter and towards the practical teachings of religion which can be found in Chapters 1 and 5. We should concentrate on removing the arrow of suffering, as the Buddha describes in his reply to Malunkyaputta, rather than asking questions about the nature of the arrow. It is from the teaching of the Great Teachers, the founders of the world religions, the Buddhas, that we obtain the practical instructions that are necessary.

The Nature of Buddhahood

In summarizing the above sections, we may say that Bahá'u'lláh's teachings agree with the Lord Buddha's in stating that it is impossible for humanity to obtain a complete knowledge of Absolute Reality. It is also not spiritually profitable to spend a great deal of time in thinking about these matters. Instead we should look to the Buddhas, who are the only source of our knowledge of the Absolute, and try to follow their teachings. We should put aside questions of the kind 'What is the nature of the Absolute Reality that stands behind the Buddhas?' and instead look to the guidance of the Buddhas. The Buddha himself suggests this:

> Since a Tathagata, even when present, is unknowable, it is inept to say of him – the Uttermost Person, the Supernal Person, the Attainer of the Supernal; that after dying the Tathagata is, or is not, or both is and is not, or neither is nor is not.[45]

And so, although the Buddha speaks of the Absolute Reality and of himself as the discloser of the Path, the *Dhamma*, and Bahá'u'lláh speaks of God and of himself as the Manifestation of God, they are in effect saying the same thing and referring to the same spiritual truth: that there is a Higher Truth, an Absolute Reality, to which human beings have no direct access. No words of description adequately apply to that reality. We can, however, know the Buddhas that come to the world. They are the intermediaries between us and the Truth. They are fully familiar with the Truth.[46] We can follow their guidance. They lead us to liberation and salvation.

There is a widespread belief that the Lord Buddha was a man like any other who attained enlightenment through his own efforts. However, if the Buddhist scriptures are examined with a fresh and unbiased eye, it is hard to come to such an understanding. For example, when asked whether he could guide people to that higher reality, Gautama Buddha replied:

> If a man had been born and brought up in (the town of)

Manasakata, every road that leads to Manasakata would be perfectly familiar to him . . . To the Tathagata, when asked touching the path which leads to the world of Brahma, there can be no doubt of difficulty. For Brahma, I know, and the world of Brahma, and the path which leadeth unto it. Yea, I know it even as one who has entered the Brahma world, and has been born within it!47

Thus the Buddhist scriptures appear to suggest that the Buddhas are in reality people of a higher plane who are temporarily in this world to guide us. Furthermore, Lord Buddha condemns any of his followers who claim that his teaching is something that the Buddha devised himself, as result of his own efforts:

Whoever, Sariputta, knowing that it is so of me, seeing that it is so, should speak thus: 'There are no suprahuman states, no excellent cognition and insight . . . in the recluse Gautama; the recluse Gautama teaches *Dhamma* on a system of his own devising beaten out by reasoning and based on investigation' – if he does not retract that speech, Sariputta, if he does not cast out that view, he is verily consigned to Niraya Hell for this sin.48

When asked about the way to attain a state of union with Brahma, Gautama Buddha replied:

Know, Vasettha, that (from time to time) a Tathagata is born into the world, a fully Enlightened One, blessed and worthy, abounding in wisdom and goodness, happy, with knowledge of the world, unsurpassed as a guide to erring mortals, a teacher of gods and men, a Blessed Buddha. He, by himself, thoroughly understands, and sees, as it were, face to face this universe – the world below with all its spirits, and the worlds above, of Mara and of Brahma – and all creatures, Samanas and Brahmins, gods and men, and he makes this knowledge known to others. The truth doth he proclaim both in its letter and in its spirit, lovely in its origin, lovely in its progress, lovely in its consummation: the higher life doth he make known, in all its purity and in all its perfectness.[49]

Thus it is clear that it was not just the attainment to enlightenment (a condition that many mortals can reach) which marked out the Buddha as extraordinary. He had been extraordinary from birth; he was from birth onwards a special order of being, which comes but rarely to the world.

Indeed, contrary to the common view that anyone can achieve enlightenment through his own efforts, the Lord Buddha asserts that it is only through the coming of a Buddha that the path is made clear and the Four Noble Truths are made known:

> So long as a Tathagata arises not, an Arahat, a Buddha Supreme, there is no shining forth of great light, of great radiance, but gross darkness, the darkness of bewilderment, prevails, and there is no proclamation of the Four Noble Truths, no teaching, no showing forth, no setting up, no opening up, no analysis, no making plain.
>
> But, brethren, as soon as a Tathagata arises in the world, then is there a shining forth of great light, of great radiance. Then is there no more gloom and darkness of bewilderment; then is there a proclamation of the Four Noble Truths; then is there teaching, a shining forth, a setting up, an opening up, an analysis, a making plain.[50]

Bahá'u'lláh expresses these same truths in his writings. He says that the Tathagatas or Manifestations of God are the intermediaries between the highest reality and this world. They are thoroughly familiar with the highest reality and can show us human beings the path to that world.

> To every discerning and illuminated heart it is evident that God, the unknowable Essence, the Divine Being, is immensely exalted beyond every human attribute, such as corporeal existence, ascent and descent, egress and regress. Far be it from His glory that human tongue

should adequately recount His praise, or that human heart comprehend His fathomless mystery. He is, and hath ever been, veiled in the ancient eternity of His Essence, and will remain in His Reality everlastingly hidden from the sight of men . . .

The door of the knowledge of the Ancient of Days being thus closed in the face of all beings, the Source of infinite grace . . . hath caused those luminous Gems of Holiness to appear out of the realm of the spirit, in the noble form of the human temple, and be made manifest unto all men, that they may impart unto the world the mysteries of the unchangeable Being, and tell of the subtleties of His imperishable Essence.[51]

Although the Buddha is one who has reached *Nibbana*, it is not true that anyone who reaches *Nibbana* is automatically a Buddha. For the statements of the Buddha indicate that while there are many who will reach *Nibbana* – thus, for example, on his deathbed, the Buddha assured all five hundred of his companions that they were stream-winners (that is, would reach *Nibbana*)[52] – fully-enlightened Buddhas who are Tathagatas and who renew the *Dhamma* and bring new teachings for the *Vinaya* come but rarely. In the Buddhist scriptures it is stated that 'Rarely do Tathagatas arise in the world, they who are Arahats, fully-enlightened ones'.[53] Indeed, the Buddha specifically states that his station is one to 'which no worldling can attain'[54] and, as we have seen, is unknowable: 'Since a Tathagata, even when actually present, is unknowable, it is inept to say of him – the Uttermost Person, the Supernal Person, the Attainer of the Supernal.'[55] Since the Tathagata or Buddha 'knows the straight path that leads to union with Brahma',[56] his function is to 'show the way'.[57]

The Buddha is to be distinguished from others who are freed by insight. The Buddha is one who brings into being a new *Dhamma*:

The Tathagata, brethren, who, being *Arahant,* is fully enlightened, he it is who doth cause a way to arise which had not arisen before; who doth proclaim a way not proclaimed before; who is the knower of a way, who understandeth a way, who is skilled in a way. And now, brethren, his disciples are wayfarers who follow after him. That, brethren, is the distinction, the specific feature which distinguishes the Tathagata who, being Arahat, is fully enlightened, from the brother who is freed by insight.[58]

The station of a Buddha is thus very exalted and a phenomenon that occurs but rarely in the world. Gautama Buddha named only three previous Buddhas in this aeon as well as Metteyya (Maitreya) Buddha who was to come after him.

Broadly speaking, Bahá'u'lláh describes the station and function of the fully-enlightened ones very similarly. He also states that such figures arise but rarely, some five hundred to one thousand years separating each from the next. Their station is very exalted, far above that of any human being, and their function is to guide humanity into the true path, to re-establish the Path of *Dhamma*, and to give new rules for humanity's social relations.

Bahá'u'lláh states that all of these great Teachers who have arisen in the past and will come in the future take on the role of intermediaries between an unknowable Absolute Reality and human beings. In one aspect they are perfect manifestations of the Absolute Reality, they are the personalized aspect of the Absolute. The Buddhas are the only contact that we in this world of *Samsara* can have with Eternity and the Absolute. As Gautama Buddha says: 'All things indeed pass away, but the Buddhas are forever in eternity.'[59] Similarly, Bahá'u'lláh writes: 'All on the earth shall pass away, but the face of thy Lord . . .'[60]

The Buddhas are the embodiments of the Truth, the Absolute, in this world. Indeed, the Buddhas have discouraged us from seeking the Absolute Truth which is beyond our ability to reach; they have instead encouraged us to look to the Buddhas themselves as the Truth. Since the Buddhas are the embodiments of the Absolute Truth, they are all that human beings are capable of understanding of the Truth. The Lord Buddha states: 'Whoever sees *Dhamma* sees me, whoever sees me sees *Dhamma*.'[61] Similarly, Bahá'u'lláh says:

> Know verily that whenever this Youth turneth His eyes towards His own self, he findeth it the most insignificant of all creation. When He contemplates, however, the bright effulgences He hath been empowered to manifest, lo, that self is transfigured before Him into a sovereign Potency permeating the essence of all things visible and invisible.[62]

These Divine Teachers who appear in the world from age to age are likened by Bahá'u'lláh to mirrors which reflect to this world the light of the Absolute. Without them, 'there is', in the words of the Buddha, 'no shining forth of great light, of great radiance, but gross darkness, the darkness of bewilderment, prevails.'[63]

The Progressive Unfoldment of the *Dhamma*

There is, however, a paradox in that the Buddha states that the Tathagata is one 'who doth cause a way to arise which had not arisen before; who doth proclaim a way not proclaimed before',[64] and yet elsewhere states that the *Dhamma* that he brings is an ancient *Dhamma*, preached by previous Buddhas:

> Even so, brethren, have I seen an ancient Path, an ancient track traversed by the Perfectly Enlightened Ones of the past. And what, brethren, is that ancient Path? It is the Noble Eightfold Path.[65]

Bahá'u'lláh makes very much the same sort of statements,

saying both that 'this is the changeless Faith of God, eternal in the past, eternal in the future'[66] and that he has brought new teachings suitable for the present-day condition of humanity.

Bahá'u'lláh has explained why the Buddha can at once state that he has proclaimed a Way that has never arisen before and at the same time assert that he teaches an ancient *Dhamma* which the former Buddhas preached. Bahá'u'lláh explains that there are two aspects to the teachings of all Buddhas. The first part consists of the spiritual and ethical teachings. These do not change from one age to another. They are preached by every Buddha that has ever come to earth. They are the ancient *Dhamma* preached by the Buddhas of old. For example, in introducing his book the *Hidden Words* (a book that is very similar to the *Dhammapada* in many ways), Bahá'u'lláh writes:

This is that which hath descended from the realm of glory, uttered by the tongue of power and might, and revealed unto the Prophets of old. We have taken the inner essence thereof and clothed it in the garment of brevity . . .[67]

Thus Bahá'u'lláh also preaches this ancient *Dhamma*. A comparison of the Buddha's rendering of the ancient *Dhamma* and Bahá'u'lláh's teaching showing how similar they are can be found in Chapter 1.

The second part of the Buddha's teaching consists of the social teachings which are designed to establish a society in which the spiritual and ethical teachings can best be put into effect. Since humanity's social condition is constantly changing and evolving, however, this aspect of the teaching changes from one Buddha to the next. It is this part of his teaching which was new with Gautama Buddha and which is progressively unfolded with each Buddha that comes. Gautama Buddha left his disciples the rules of the *Sangha*, the *Vinaya*, as the best way for spiritual progress at that time. Today Bahá'u'lláh has brought a new social teaching and a new *Vinaya* which is set out in Chapters 5 and 6. Bahá'u'lláh states that this is now the best way of achieving spiritual progress for individuals and a peaceful society.

The line of Buddhas have each come to the world one after the other with an interval of hundreds or thousands of years between them. Gautama Buddha teaches that he was not the first Buddha upon the earth, nor would he be the last.[68] Bahá'u'lláh agrees with this statement. Indeed, such figures as Zoroaster, Moses, Jesus, Muḥammad and the Hindu *Avatars* such as Krishna have all come to the world to bring enlightenment. Bahá'u'lláh states that he is one of these figures and predicts the coming of a further Buddha or Manifestation in another one thousand years.

We are told by Gautama Buddha that we should not try to make any distinctions between the Buddhas for they are all in essence one. In the Buddhist commentaries it is written, for example:

> There is no distinction between any of the Buddhas in physical beauty, moral habit, concentration, wisdom, cognition and insight of freedom, the four confidences, the ten powers of a Tathagata, the six special cognitions, the fourteen cognitions of Buddhas, eighteen Buddha-*dhammas*, in a word in all the *dhammas* of Buddhas, for all Buddhas are exactly the same as regards Buddha-*dhammas*.[69]

Bahá'u'lláh makes exactly the same statement:

> Beware . . . lest ye be tempted to make any distinction between any of the Manifestations of His Cause, or to discriminate against the signs that have accompanied and proclaimed their Revelation . . . Whoso maketh the slightest possible difference between their persons, their words, their messages, their acts and manners, hath indeed disbelieved in God, hath repudiated His signs, and betrayed the Cause of His Messengers.[70]

In their other aspect, however, there are differences

between the Buddhas. The Buddhas pertain to the phenomenal world and are subject to its limitations. They each arise at a particular time in history and their arising accords with the needs and circumstances of their time. Each of these Buddhas (or Manifestations, as Bahá'u'lláh refers to them) have

> ... a distinct individuality, a definitely prescribed mission, a predestined Revelation, and specially designated limitations. Each one of them is known by a different name, is characterized by a special attribute, fulfils a definite Mission, and is entrusted with a particular Revelation.[71]

For example, the mission of Lord Buddha was to clarify and reform the degenerate practices and beliefs that existed among the Hindus of his time. He stopped the custom of animal sacrifice which had existed up to that time. He taught the everyday practice of a religious way of life by each person rather than the practice of rituals and superstitions.

The mission of Bahá'u'lláh as the Metteyya Buddha is different from that of the Buddha. The world is now in a different state and a different set of social teachings is necessary. The mission of Bahá'u'lláh is to regenerate the religious belief of all humanity and to unite all mankind. Thus Bahá'u'lláh has unfolded for humanity new social teachings, a new social *Dhamma*, in order to bring this about. It was not possible for Gautama Buddha to give such teachings because the people of his time would not have been able to understand his message if he had given a teaching about world unity. It is likely that at that time most people's perception of the world did not extend beyond their own village. Today, however, we have the capacity to understand such concepts and so the new Buddha, Bahá'u'lláh, has brought these teachings.

This not to say that the Buddha did not have the same knowledge that Bahá'u'lláh has; all of the Buddhas are supremely-enlightened and have full knowledge of all *Dhamma*. But even as the Buddha stated, the knowledge that he taught was just a small fraction of his total knowledge. The Buddha explained this in the parable of the Simsapa leaves:

> Once the Exalted One was staying at Kosambi in a Simsapa Grove. Then the Exalted One, gathering up a few Simsapa leaves in his hands, said to the monks: 'What do you think, monks? Which are more numerous, just this mere handful of Simsapa leaves I have here, or those in the grove overhead?'
>
> 'Very few in number, Lord, are the leaves in the handful gathered up by the Exalted One: much more in number are those in the grove overhead.'
>
> 'Just so, monks, much more in number are those things I have found out, but not revealed; very few are the things I have revealed.'[72]

The Buddha goes on to say that he has only revealed that which would be of spiritual profit for the people of his time. Bahá'u'lláh teaches that all of the Buddhas in every age possess all knowledge but they skilfully and carefully adapt the knowledge that they give to the needs and capacities of the people of their age.

The Pathways to Salvation or Liberation (*Nibbana*)

The main purpose of a *Dhamma* is to show human beings how to achieve *Nibbana*. The religions of the world have emphasized two main pathways to salvation or liberation. The first of these is faith. This pathway can be found in Christianity, for example, where salvation is considered to be attained through faith in Jesus Christ. There are also some elements of such an approach to *Nibbana* in Mahayana Buddhism: attainment to *Nibbana* depends upon faith in the saving power of Amida Buddha in the Pure Land sects of Japanese Buddhism, for example. The second pathway to salvation or liberation is that of deeds and effort. This is the pathway emphasized in Theravada Buddhism.

We have seen above, in Chapter 1, that the Bahá'í teachings also stress the importance of one's individual efforts to achieve one's own salvation or liberation. In fact, in the Bahá'í scriptures, both of these pathways are considered important. Both faith and individual effort are necessary for the achievement of salvation or liberation. What is needed is 'first, conscious knowledge, and second, the practice of good deeds'.[73] The spiritual state of human beings depends upon both 'their faith and their conduct'.[74]

Although Theravada Buddhism has been advocated as a religion of reason and systematic practical procedures, there is evidence from the books of the Tripitaka that the early Buddhist community also attached great importance to faith and devotion in initiating and developing the religious life. Faith (*saddha*, placing one's heart on) is frequently described as being the essential step in the going forth from home into homelessness; that is, the adopting of the monastic life and joining the *Sangha*.[75] On many occasions, individuals are described thus: 'Having heard the Buddha's teachings, he acquired faith in the Tathagata.'[76] This faith then leads him to go forth into homelessness, follow the Eightfold Path and eventually achieve *Nibbana*.[77] Conversely, the Buddha condemns those who do not go forth 'out of faith' as 'impostors, frauds, deceivers, who are vainly puffed up', etc.[78] Thus it is that faith is referred to as the seed of all wholesome states, ready to grow.[79] The Brahmin Unabha is praised as one whose faith is said to be 'strong, not to be uprooted by any recluse or brahmin or deva or Mara or Brahma, or by anyone else in the world.'[80]

The Buddhist scriptures even indicate that in some cases the Buddha infused the mind of some of his followers with faith. Roja the Malla had met the Buddha but evinced no interest in his teachings until the Buddha infused Roja's mind with love and he acquired faith in the Buddha.[81] The concept that the conditions for faith provided by the Buddha through what could be considered to be a gracious activity is also found in the Bahá'í texts in connection with Bahá'u'lláh. [82]

Lord Buddha urges, however, a critical and rational faith (*akaravati saddha*), not a blind, groundless faith (*amulika saddha*). Indeed, the Buddha strongly condemns a blind faith based merely on custom, traditions and the reports of others; rather he urges a faith based on seeing and knowing for oneself, on striving for certain knowledge.[83] Such a critical faith is considered by the Buddha to be grounded in awareness and understanding.[84] In the Bahá'í writings also, faith is not blind faith; rather it is described as 'discerning faith' and linked to knowledge and understanding.[85]

The modern secular view is that faith is something that confines and limits the human being. Both the Buddhist and the Bahá'í scriptures agree that faith, far from being this, is in fact the path to liberation:

> By Faith you shall be free and go beyond the realm of death.
>
> *Suttanipata*[86]

> . . . whosoever partook of the cup of love, obtained his portion of the ocean of eternal grace and of the showers of everlasting mercy, and entered into the life of faith – the heavenly and everlasting life.
>
> Bahá'u'lláh, *Book of Certitude*[87]

Magic, Spirits and Ghosts

Many people have a fear of evil spirits and ghosts. They go to great lengths to try to ward off the effects of such spirits, particularly through the use of magic spells and amulets. Indeed, for some people this becomes the main part of their religion. The Bahá'í Faith teaches that we should not live in such fear of evil spirits. Evil exists only as the absence of good. Good is far more powerful than evil and can overcome it. Human beings have both a higher good side and a lower evil side to them. In some people this lower side takes control and leads them into evil acts. The purpose of religion is to develop the good side which is present in all human beings.

In particular, what are considered to be the works of evil spirits are often just the effects of the human mind. Although the Bahá'í teachings acknowledge that spirits, which are the souls of people who have died, exist, we are instructed not to try to communicate with them. If we concentrate our attentions on such matters, we are delaying our spiritual development. Magic and contact with spirits and ghosts are not the ways forward to spiritual development and human contentment. Only following of the path described by the Buddha and Bahá'u'lláh will protect us from evil and ensure our spiritual progress.

3

Prophecies of the Buddha

Bahá'ís consider Bahá'u'lláh to be the fulfilment of the Buddha's prophecy that, in due time, another Buddha would come to the world, the Metteyya (or Maitreya) Buddha. The Buddha prophesied:

> At that period, brethren, there will arise in the world an Exalted One named Metteyya, Arahat, Fully Awakened, abounding in wisdom and goodness, happy, with knowledge of the worlds, unsurpassed as a guide to mortals willing to be led, a teacher for gods and men, an Exalted One, a Buddha, even as I am now. He, by himself, will thoroughly know and see, as it were face to face, this universe, with its worlds of the spirits, its Brahmas and its Maras, and its world of recluses and brahmins, of princes and peoples, even as I now, by myself, thoroughly know and see them.
>
> *Digha Nikaya*[1]

> The truth [the Norm, the Dhamma], lovely in its origin, lovely in its progress, lovely in its consummation, will he (Metteyya Buddha) proclaim, both in the spirit and in the letter; the higher life will he make known, in all its fullness and in all its purity, even as I do now. He will be accompanied by a congregation of some thousands of brethren, even as I am now accompanied by a congregation of some hundreds of brethren.
>
> *Digha Nikaya*[2]

This prophecy of Gautama Buddha clearly predicts that the teaching of Metteyya Buddha will apply to a much larger part of the world than his own teaching – in other words that it will be a worldwide teaching. Indeed, Bahá'u'lláh's teaching is precisely that, for Bahá'ís believe that Bahá'u'lláh does not just fulfil the Buddhist prophecies. They claim that he is also for the Jews the expected Messiah, for Christians and Muslims the awaited return of Christ, for the Zoroastrians (Parsees) the Saoshyant, for the Hindus the Kalki Avatar, as well as being for Buddhists the Metteyya Buddha. The prophecy of the Lord Buddha that the teaching of Metteyya Buddha will be much more extensive than his own is already being fulfilled through the Bahá'í Faith, already a worldwide religion with communities in every part of the planet consisting of all the races and nations of humanity.

So what is this 'teaching that is lovely' predicted by Gautama Buddha and which Bahá'ís believe Bahá'u'lláh has brought? It is the renewed spiritual guidance and the new social teachings given by Bahá'u'lláh, which we will examine in Chapter 5.

But there is another prophecy that is much more specific about the time of the coming of the Metteyya Buddha. Sariputta asked the Buddha:

'The Hero that shall follow you
As Buddha of what sort is he?
The account in full I fain would learn.
Declare to me, thou Seeing One.'
Gautama Buddha replied:

'I will tell you, Sariputta
Pray lend your ears, for I will speak.
In this auspicious aeon
'Three leaders have already lived
Kakusandha, Konagamana
And also the leader Kassapa.

'The Buddha Supreme, now am I
But after me Metteyya comes,
Before this auspicious aeon
Runs to the end of its years.

'This Buddha, then, Metteyya by name
Supreme, and of all men the chief . . .'

Sariputta: 'How will it occur?'

Buddha: 'After my decease, first will occur the five disappearances. And what are the five disappearances?'
    'The disappearance of attainments [to *nibbana*], the dis-
appearance of the method [inability to practise wisdom,
insight and the four purities of moral habit], the disappearance of learning [loss of men who follow the *Dhamma*
and the forgetting of the Pitakas and other scriptures], the
disappearance of the symbols [the loss of the outward
forms, the robes and practices of monkhood], the disappearance of the relics [the *Dhātu*] . . .
    'Then when the Dispensation of the Perfect Buddha is
5000 years old, the relics, not receiving reverence and
honour, will go to places where they can receive them . . .
This, Sariputta, is called the disappearance of relics.'[3]

This passage clearly shows that the Metteyya Buddha will
appear 'before this auspicious aeon runs to the end of its
years'. Since Gautama Buddha appeared in India and was
speaking to disciples who had also been Hindus and were
familiar with the Hindu system of dating cycles, it would
seem likely that when Gautama Buddha said 'before this
auspicious aeon runs to the end of its years', he was speaking of the Hindu Kali Yuga in the middle of which he had
appeared. This Kali Yuga ended at noon on 1 August 1943,
equivalent to the year 2486 of the Buddhist Era. Therefore
according to this prophecy of the Buddha, the Metteyya
Buddha should already have appeared sometime before
1943.[4]
    It is true that this prophecy of the Five Disappearances

49

states that the last of the Disappearances will occur when the Dispensation of the Buddha is five thousand years old. Since only 2,500 years have passed, it might seem that it is not yet time for the coming of Metteyya Buddha. It should, however, be borne in mind that when the Buddha allowed women to be ordained as nuns, he then prophesied that because of this the time that the *Dhamma* endured would be halved. The period during which the full *Dhamma* is known and *Nibbana* achieved (the First Disappearance) is halved from one thousand years to five hundred[5] and similarly for the whole process, thus resulting in 2,500 years during which all of the Five Disappearances must occur. The year 2500 of the Buddhist Era was celebrated in AD 1956. This ties in very well with AD 1943 as the last possible date for the appearance of the Metteyya Buddha.[6] Bahá'ís believe that Bahá'u'lláh, who appeared in the century before the expiration of this deadline, was the Metteyya Buddha.

The Five Disappearances refer to the gradual disappearance of the *Dhamma* from the world. This is something which the Buddha knew would happen since everything in this world is transient and changes. He describes the gradual fading of the efficacy of his teachings until even the 'true sacred relics (*Dhātu*), not receiving reverence and honour, will go to places where they can receive them'.[7] If we consider the situation in the Buddhist world at the time of the advent of Bahá'u'lláh in the middle of the nineteenth century, we will note that all of this prophecy had been fulfilled by that time. Buddhism had disappeared from its native soil in India; the sacred relics had gone from India 'to places where they can receive' reverence and honour in Sri Lanka, Burma, Thailand and elsewhere in the Buddhist world. The scripture and the *Dhamma* could even be said to have disappeared from the Buddhist community; when Colonel Olcott arrived in Sri Lanka in the last half of the nineteenth century, he could find no monks who knew Pali and could read the scriptures. There has, of course, been a revival in Buddhism since those days but this is only to be expected. For with the appearance of a new Buddha, Bahá'u'lláh, in the world, the light is once more shining; and the sun, when it shines, shines on all things, whether or not they are turned to it.

Even today in Buddhist countries, however, it is difficult to apply the laws of the *Sangha* as given in the Buddhist scriptures. Monks, for example, rarely now join the *Sangha* for life: many leave and get married; even when in the *Sangha*, many are forced to carry money with them, some are involved in politics, and so forth.

Gautama Buddha described the degraded state of the world at the time of the coming of Metteyya; these conditions have been fulfilled today:

> Thus, brethren, from goods not being bestowed on the destitute, poverty grew great . . . stealing . . . violence . . . murder . . . lying . . . evil speaking . . . adultery . . . abusive and idle talk . . . covetousness and ill-will . . . false opinions . . . incest, wanton greed and perverted lust . . . till finally lack of filial and religious piety and lack of regard for the head of the clan grew great. From these things growing, the life-span of those beings and the comeliness of them wasted . . .
>
> Among such humans, the ten moral courses of conduct will disappear, the ten immoral courses of action will flourish excessively; there will be no word for moral among such humans – far less any moral agent. Among such humans, brethren, they who lack filial and religious piety, and show no respect for the head of the clan – it is they to whom homage and praise will be given, just as today praise and homage are given to the filial-minded, to the pious and to them who respect the heads of their clans . . .
>
> The world will fall into promiscuity, like goats and sheep, fowls and swine, dogs and jackals.
>
> Among such humans, brethren, keen mutual enmity will

become the rule, keen ill-will, keen animosity, passionate
thoughts even of killing, in a mother towards her child, in
a child towards its mother, in a father towards his child
and a child towards its father, in brother to brother, in
brother to sister, in sister to brother . . .[8]

As indicated in this prophecy, the *Dhamma* will have disappeared from the world by this time. Gautama Buddha
states that the true *Dhamma* will not disappear from the
world until a false *Dhamma* appears to replace it.

There is no disappearing of the true *Dhamma* until a
counterfeit *dhamma* arises in the world. Once a counterfeit *dhamma* arises then there is a disappearing of the
true *Dhamma*. It is when, here in the Order itself, hollow
and foolish persons arise that they make this true
Dhamma disappear.[9]

Bahá'u'lláh has confirmed that this false, counterfeit
Dhamma is present in the world and is replacing the true
Dhamma. In the Bahá'í writings it is stated that the true
Dhamma has been replaced by a desire for material things:

Today, all the peoples of the world are indulging in self-
interest and exert the utmost effort and endeavour to
promote their own material interests. They are worship-
ping themselves and not the divine reality, nor the world
of mankind. They seek diligently their own benefit and not
the common weal. This is because they are captives of the
world of nature and unaware of the divine teachings, of
the bounty of the Kingdom and of the Sun of Truth.[10]

These prophecies appear to describe accurately the present
condition of the world with its materialism, consumerism,
promiscuity, drug problems and increasing violence and
conflict. These problems are ravaging every society and
undermining the pillars of all social structures. The way in
which this situation can be remedied is, as the prophecy
indicates, for a new Buddha to arise. Only a new Buddha

can restore the *Dhamma* and replace the counterfeit *Dhamma* of materialism and selfishness; only a new Buddha can give the new teachings to solve the social problems of the world; only a new Buddha can solve the problems caused by the modern world for the laws of the *Sangha* by giving new laws. Bahá'ís believe that Bahá'u'lláh is the Metteyya Buddha prophesied by Lord Buddha and has done all of these things.

4

The Life of Bahá'u'lláh

Bahá'u'lláh is the founder of the Bahá'í Faith. Bahá'ís believe that he is a fully-enlightened one whose mission is to guide humanity in the present age in which we live. His role is likened to that of a doctor who has the remedy for the illness of the world and the suffering of human beings or to a teacher who has come to educate humanity in teachings that are suited for this age.

The Life of Bahá'u'lláh

As mentioned in Chapter 2, according to Bahá'í belief, in the lives of the fully-enlightened ones certain personality types return and certain key events and attitudes are re-enacted. Therefore it is not surprising that there should be some similarities between the life of Bahá'u'lláh and the life of the Buddha.

Bahá'u'lláh, like Gautama Buddha, was born into an ancient and royal family. His family traced its ancestry back to the original Aryan peoples who settled in Iran and India. It was, according to various traditions, from these peoples that the Indian *Avatars*, such as Rama and Krishna, the Buddha as well as the Persian prophet Zoroaster were descended.

Bahá'u'lláh's birth occurred in BE 2362 (AD 1817) in Tehran, Iran. Many prodigies and wonders are recorded of all of the Buddhas or Manifestations of God. This was also the case with Bahá'u'lláh. For example, on one occasion, while still a child, he appeared before the king to argue a case on behalf of his father.

Although Bahá'u'lláh was raised surrounded by luxuries of every description, his own inclination was to turn away from these and to seek out a religious life. When Bahá'u'lláh was a young man there arose in Iran a movement begun by another young Iranian called the Báb, the Bábí movement. It holds a very special place in Bahá'í history. This is because the Báb taught the people that a new divine teacher was about to appear in the world and that all should prepare themselves for this. This was of course a prophecy of the coming of Bahá'u'lláh. Bahá'ís regard the Báb as a divine teacher in his own right and the Bábí movement to be the forerunner of the Bahá'í Faith. As a result, Bahá'ís date the start of their religion from the year in which the Báb announced his mission, BE 2387 (AD 1844).

When he was aged 25 Bahá'u'lláh heard of the message of the Báb, who was causing a stir throughout the country. Bahá'u'lláh accepted the Báb's teachings and arose to help the new cause. In doing so he was turning his back on all of his family's wealth and position in society, as did the Buddha. Opposition to the new religion arose from the established religious leaders of the time who persecuted the followers of the Báb. Because of these persecutions Bahá'u'lláh himself suffered greatly. Eventually he was imprisoned in the a dungeon called the Síyáh-Chál (Black Pit) in Tehran.

It was in this unlikely setting of the Black Pit that Bahá'u'lláh experienced his enlightenment – the equivalent of the Buddha's enlightenment under the Bo (Bodhi) Tree. He describes this experience thus:

> During the days I lay in the prison of Ṭihrán, though the galling weight of the chains and the stench-filled air allowed Me but little sleep, still in those infrequent moments of slumber I felt as if something flowed from the crown of My head over My breast, even as a mighty torrent

that precipitateth itself upon the earth from the summit of a lofty mountain. Every limb of My body would, as a result, be set afire. At such moments My tongue recited what no man could bear to hear.[1]

After being released from imprisonment, Bahá'u'lláh was forced to travel into exile. The Buddha spent much of his ministry travelling from place to place and Bahá'u'lláh spent his ministry in different places of exile. In each place a group of his followers gathered around him and he taught them.

The first place to which Bahá'u'lláh was exiled was Baghdad, which is now the capital of Iraq. Here he was surrounded by much evil behaviour by other followers of the Báb and he left to go out to the mountains of Sulaymáníyyih.

It is recorded that when the Buddha first achieved enlightenment, he looked around him. When he saw 'the world lost in low views and confused efforts, thickly covered with the dirt of the passions, and saw on the other hand the exceeding subtlety of the *Dhamma* of emancipation, he felt inclined to take no action. But when he weighed up the significance of the pledge to enlighten all beings that he had taken in the past, he became again more favourable to the idea of proclaiming the path to Peace.'[2] Similarly, Bahá'u'lláh writes that when he left Baghdad and went up into the mountains of Sulaymáníyyih, he felt inclined to remain there: 'Our withdrawal contemplated no return, and Our separation hoped for no reunion.'[3] But eventually, realizing that unless he returned there was no way for the people to achieve enlightenment and all the sufferings endured by the Báb would have been in vain, he decided to go back:

But for My recognition of the fact that the blessed Cause of the Primal Point [the Báb] was on the verge of being completely obliterated, and all the sacred blood . . . would have been shed in vain, I would in no wise have consented to return to the people of the Bayán [the followers of the Báb], and would have abandoned them to the worship of the idols their imaginations had fashioned.[4]

These events have parallels in the life of the Buddha. When the Buddha was in Kosambi there was a dispute between two factions among the Bhikkus, the monks who accompanied him. He tried to settle this dispute but failed. In disgust, and unknown to anyone, he secretly left for the jungle of Parileyya. Eventually he was found, and at the request of his chief disciple Ananda, agreed to return to Jethawanaramaya, where the disputing factions met and apologized to him.

When he returned to Baghdad from Sulaymáníyyih, Bahá'u'lláh began to rebuild the Bábí community. Many of the Bábís of Iran travelled to Baghdad to hear his teaching. Finally, in 1863, the governments of Iran and Turkey, worried by Bahá'u'lláh's growing influence agreed to exile him to another place.

As he was leaving Baghdad, Bahá'u'lláh gathered some of his followers in a garden outside Baghdad called the Garden of Riḍván. He told them that, just as the Báb had foretold (and long before that the Buddha had prophesied this also – see Chapter 3), this age was to see the fulfilment of the prophecies of all of the religions of the world. He, Bahá'u'lláh, was this fulfilment, the Promised One of all religions.

Bahá'u'lláh began to teach his message, at first only to the other followers of the Báb, but later openly to all people. He soon had a following of many thousands. Many of these travelled thousands of miles to see him in the distant places of exile.

One factor in the teachings of Bahá'u'lláh that is very similar to that of the Buddha is the severe condemnation of the religious leaders of the day. The Buddha was very critical of

the Brahmins of his time. In particular, he denounces those
who set themselves up as spiritual guides on the Path, but
who, in reality, have no knowledge of the Path and who live
lives that are not conducive to progress along the spiritual
Path. He likens these to the blind leading the blind[5] and
calls them worse than dogs in some respects.[6] Bahá'u'lláh
is similarly critical of the religious leaders of his time. He
asserts that each time one of the great Enlightened Ones,
the founders of the world's religions, has come to the world,
it has been mainly the religious leaders who, out of fear for
their own position and status, have opposed him.
Bahá'u'lláh condemns:

> . . . the divines and doctors living in the days of the
> Manifestation of God, who, because of their want of dis-
> cernment and their love and eagerness for leadership,
> have failed to submit to the Cause of God, nay, have even
> refused to incline their ears unto the divine Melody . . .
> And the people also . . . taking them for their masters,
> have placed themselves unreservedly under the authority
> of these pompous and hypocritical leaders, for they have
> no sight, no hearing, no heart, of their own to distinguish
> truth from falsehood.
>
> Notwithstanding the divinely-inspired admonitions of
> all the Prophets, the Saints, and Chosen ones of God,
> enjoining the people to see with their own eyes and hear
> with their own ears, they have disdainfully rejected their
> counsels and have blindly followed, and will continue to
> follow, the leaders of their Faith . . .
>
> It is clear and evident that whenever the Manifestations
> of Holiness were revealed, the divines of their day have
> hindered the people from attaining unto the way of truth.
> To this testify the records of all the scriptures and heav-
> enly books. Not one Prophet of God was made manifest
> Who did not fall a victim to the relentless hate, to the
> denunciation, denial, and execration of the clerics of His
> day! Woe unto them for the iniquities their hands have

formerly wrought! Woe unto them for that which they are now doing! What veils of glory more grievous than these embodiments of error! By the righteousness of God! to pierce such veils is the mightiest of all acts, and to rend them asunder the most meritorious of all deeds![7]

It was undoubtedly partly because of Bahá'u'lláh's success in attracting disciples that the religious leaders of the day showed such great envy and hatred towards him. In the same way, it was the attraction of the people to the Buddha that led many of the religious leaders and holy men of his time to oppose him.

As with Siddharta Buddha, the opposition that was most hurtful, however, was to come from within Bahá'u'lláh's own family. With the Buddha, it was his cousin Devadatta who, as a result of his jealousy at the position attained by the Gautama Buddha, committed two of the Five Deadly Sins: he caused a split in the ranks of the Buddha's followers and tried to kill the Buddha. In the case of Bahá'u'lláh, it was his half-brother Mírzá Yaḥyá who, also out of jealousy, committed the same offences. Although already occupying a respected position within the movement, he rose up against Bahá'u'lláh and tried to split the community by setting up an alternative leadership. Having failed in that, he then tried to poison Bahá'u'lláh.

Despite these setbacks, Bahá'u'lláh continued to teach the Path of *Dhamma* and the means for attaining both individual and social enlightenment. He succeeded in gathering many followers. The kings and governments of the time tried to silence his teaching. They exiled him from one place to another and imprisoned him. Finally he was sent to 'Akká on the shores of the Mediterranean Sea.

It was the intention of these kings to wipe out all traces of Bahá'u'lláh's teaching. Instead, however, his teachings spread and many pilgrims made long journeys of thousands of miles to come to 'Akká and receive his guidance.

In the end, Bahá'u'lláh's influence became so great that the governor of 'Akká could no longer keep Bahá'u'lláh in prison. He urged Bahá'u'lláh to leave the prison-city and to live where he pleased. Bahá'u'lláh spent the last years of his life in a large mansion outside 'Akká. Here he received the hundreds of pilgrims who came to see him.

When Bahá'u'lláh passed away in BE 2435 (1892 AD) he left instructions that his eldest son, 'Abdu'l-Bahá, was to be regarded by all Bahá'ís as the leader of the Bahá'í community. 'Abdu'l-Bahá was the only person authorized by Bahá'u'lláh to interpret the Bahá'í teachings. Bahá'u'lláh gave very strict instructions about this matter. This was in order that the Bahá'í Faith should not be divided into hundreds of sects as other religions are. Since the primary aim of the Bahá'í Faith is to bring about unity, Bahá'u'lláh and 'Abdu'l-Bahá devoted a great deal of time and effort to ensuring that differences and sects do not arise among the Bahá'ís as they had done among the followers of Siddharta Buddha and all the other fully-enlightened ones. They explained and established what is called the Covenant. This is an agreement that every Bahá'í enters into that he or she will not be diverted away by the opinions of others but will always look towards the Centre of the Religion for guidance.

'Abdu'l-Bahá, who died in AD 1921, in turn appointed his grandson Shoghi Effendi as the authoritative interpreter of the Bahá'í holy writings. Following the latter's death (in AD 1957), the Universal House of Justice was established in AD 1963. This is the supreme authority of the Bahá'í world and thus again prevents differences and sects arising among the Bahá'ís.

The Bahá'í World Today

The Bahá'í world has expanded very greatly, especially in

the last 30 years. There are now Bahá'ís in almost every country of the world. The structure of the Bahá'í administration is described in Chapter 5. In 1994 National Spiritual Assemblies were established in 173 countries of the world; there are now more than 20,000 Local Spiritual Assemblies and over 120,000 places where Bahá'ís reside. There are more than five million Bahá'ís in total.

Bahá'ís are active with many agencies of the United Nations. The Bahá'í International Community has consultative status with the UN's Economic and Social Council (ECOSOC) and Children's Fund (UNICEF). It is affiliated with the Environment Programme (UNEP) and various other bodies. Bahá'ís regularly participate in UN conferences on such subjects as human rights, social and economic development, narcotic drugs, disarmament, and so on.

As one may gather from the Bahá'í social principles, Bahá'ís are interested in the betterment of humankind. As a result, they are involved in a large number and variety of social and economic development projects. In 1992 there were 1,344 such projects worldwide. Most of these are educational projects, a quarter involving the setting up of simple village schools, but there are also a number of health, agricultural and community development projects.

5

The *Sangha*
The Social Teachings

If as indicated above, the ethical and moral teachings of
the Bahá'í Faith are very similar to those of Buddhism, the
questions may well be asked: what then is the difference?
why have a new teaching? Since the Path of *Dhamma* is
eternal, there seems no reason to suppose that there is any
need for a new teaching. Apart from teaching the Path of
Dhamma, however, the Buddha also gave instructions on
the best way in which human beings might organize society so as to put themselves into the best possible position
to implement the Path of *Dhamma*. These instructions he
gave in the form of his rules for the organization of the
Sangha (assembly or community). In one of his last
addresses to his disciples, the Buddha himself states that
the two great authorities after him that he is leaving to his
disciples are the *Suttas* (the teaching of the *Dhamma*) and
the Discipline (*Vinaya*) for the *Sangha*.[1]

While the Path of *Dhamma* is, as the Buddha has stated,
eternal, the laws for the organization of the *Sangha* need
to change and adapt as human society changes and evolves
over the centuries. Indeed, the Buddha himself stated that
his teaching of the *Dhamma* had been brought previously
by earlier Buddhas. What the Buddha brought which is not
recorded in the accounts of earlier Buddhas is the social
teachings for the *Sangha*. It is therefore these social teachings, the way in which the Path of *Dhamma* is to be
implemented in society, that Bahá'ís consider need reform

as the conditions of society change. Thus there is a need for a new teaching.

The Buddha lived 2500 years ago and many things have changed in the world since then, especially in the last hundred years. At the time of the Buddha men and women were required to spend long hours labouring hard in order to extract a livelihood from the earth. Therefore society could only support a relatively few people in the time-consuming tasks of becoming literate, studying the holy writings and devoting themselves to religious matters. Thus the Buddha gave instructions for the setting up of an order of monks, the *Sangha* – a few people whose vocation it would be to study the Buddhist texts, to lead the holy life and to guide the illiterate masses. Furthermore, the world in which the Buddha lived was a relatively small circumscribed area and would remain so for centuries after, so there was no need for the Buddha to give detailed instructions for social organization and interactions. He largely contented himself with giving instructions for the conduct of the monkhood.

However, we live in an entirely different situation in the world and Bahá'u'lláh's social teachings reflect this new condition. He states that all people must acquire an education – this is well within the capability of the world now. When all can read and study the holy writings for themselves, it then becomes the obligation of all to follow the Path of *Dhamma* and to seek enlightenment. Thus Bahá'u'lláh has abolished the difference between monks and lay-people and has in effect made all men monks and all women nuns. All must earn a living for themselves and their families while at the same time striving to follow the Path of *Dhamma* in their personal lives. The responsibility rests now with each individual.

Just before his Parinibbana, the Buddha spoke some final words to his disciples: 'Work out your salvation with diligence.' These words apply even more to Bahá'ís, who are instructed to be responsible for their own spiritual progress – to investigate the truth, to read the scriptures and, without the help of priests and monks, to work out their own salvation, using the path shown to them by Bahá'u'lláh. Having shown us the path, Bahá'u'lláh lays down this challenge in the last words of one of his books:

> I bear witness, O friends! that the favour is complete, the argument fulfilled, the proof manifest and the evidence established. Let it now be seen what your endeavours in the path of detachment will reveal. In this wise hath the divine favour been fully vouchsafed unto you and unto them that are in heaven and on earth.[2]

Bahá'u'lláh did not, however, leave his followers entirely alone in their attempts to follow the *Dhamma*. Although he stated that in this age neither a priesthood nor monastic orders of monks and nuns were necessary, he did give instructions for the setting up of Bahá'í communities to provide the spiritual support that had previously come from the monkhood.

Through modern technology the whole world has become physically united and it is now easier to travel from one side of the world to the other than it was to travel from one city to the neighbouring one in the time of the Buddha. Therefore Bahá'u'lláh found it necessary to give instructions for the setting up of a world community – a universal *Sangha* – through which all human beings can relate to and support one another in peace. Thus it may be said that Bahá'u'lláh's teachings consist of the eternal Path of *Dhamma* together the new social teachings for a universal *Sangha*.

Of course, many modern Buddhists have realized the need to reinterpret the teachings of the Buddha in a way that accords with the current realities of the world. Unfortunately, they disagree among themselves as to what the answer should be. Being only human, they lack the authority to make a new interpretation that will be accepted by the whole *Sangha*. Only the appearance of a new Buddha would give the necessary authority for the changes that are needed. This is what Bahá'u'lláh claims. Bahá'ís believe that Bahá'u'lláh is a new Buddha, fully enlightened with teachings for the present situation of the world. Bahá'ís believe Bahá'u'lláh to be the Metteyya Buddha whom Gautama Buddha predicted would come.

Bahá'u'lláh's teachings for a universal *Sangha* can be divided into two parts: the general social principles that must be followed to bring about a situation of peace and goodwill among the various nations, races and religions in the world; and the specific social structure that Bahá'u'lláh has instructed his followers to adopt and which they believe is the embryonic form of the universal *Sangha*.

General Social Principles

World Peace – The Unity of Humankind

Bahá'u'lláh states that the main purpose of his message is to establish the unity of the world. In the last one hundred years, through advances in science and technology, humanity has progressed to the point where the world is now physically united by modern means of travel and communication. This age is the first time in human history that the unity of the world has been a possibility.

Of course, Lord Buddha himself recognized the importance of unity. In the Maha-Parinibbana-Sutta, the Buddha's last address to his disciples, he advised them thus:

> So long, O monks, as the brethren meet together in full and frequent assemblies – so long as they meet together in concord, and rise in concord, and carry out in concord the

duties of the order . . . so long may the brethren be
expected not to decline but to prosper.[3]

In the time of the Buddha this unity could only be over a
small area. Now, in the time of the Metteyya Buddha, it
can be worldwide, just as the Buddha predicted when he
said that his own teachings would attract merely hundreds
of disciples whereas the Metteyya Buddha would attract
disciples in their thousands. 'Abdu'l-Bahá, the son of
Bahá'u'lláh, explains it thus:

> In cycles gone by, though harmony was established, yet,
> owing to the absence of means, the unity of all mankind
> could not have been achieved. Continents remained widely
> divided, nay even among the peoples of one and the same
> continent association and interchange of thought were
> wellnigh impossible. Consequently intercourse, under-
> standing and unity amongst all the peoples and kindreds
> of the earth were unattainable. In this day, however,
> means of communication have multiplied, and the five
> continents of the earth have virtually merged into one.
> And for everyone it is now easy to travel to any land, to
> associate and exchange views with its peoples, and to
> become familiar, through publications, with the condi-
> tions, the religious beliefs and the thoughts of all men. In
> like manner all the members of the human family,
> whether peoples or governments, cities or villages, have
> become increasingly interdependent. For none is self-suf-
> ficiency any longer possible, inasmuch as political ties
> unite all peoples and nations, and the bonds of trade and
> industry, of agriculture and education, are being strength-
> ened every day. Hence the unity of all mankind can in this
> day be achieved. Verily this is none other but one of the
> wonders of this wondrous age . . .[4]

And yet, the world is still very disunited at the social and
political level. Bahá'u'lláh states that this situation must
cease. Humanity must come together in unity.

The well-being of mankind, its peace and security, are unattainable unless and until its unity is firmly established.[5]

Ye are the fruits of one tree, and the leaves of one branch. Deal ye one with another with the utmost love and harmony, with friendliness and fellowship . . . So powerful is the light of unity that it can illuminate the whole earth.[6]

Among the proposals put forward by Bahá'u'lláh and now being earnestly advocated by the Bahá'ís of the world is the convening of an assembly of the nations of the world to discuss the promotion of an enduring peace.

The time must come when the imperative necessity for the holding of a vast, an all-embracing assemblage of men will be universally realized. The rulers and kings of the earth must needs attend it, and, participating in its deliberations, must consider such ways and means as will lay the foundations of the world's Great Peace amongst men. Such a peace demandeth that the Great Powers should resolve, for the sake of the tranquillity of the peoples of the earth, to be fully reconciled among themselves. Should any king take up arms against another, all should unitedly arise and prevent him. If this be done, the nations of the world will no longer require any armaments, except for the purpose of preserving the security of their realms and of maintaining internal order within their territories. This will ensure the peace and composure of every people, government and nation.[7]

O contending peoples and kindreds of the earth! Set your faces towards unity, and let the radiance of its light shine upon you. Gather ye together, and . . . resolve to root out whatever is the source of contention amongst you.[8]

Another international institution which Bahá'u'lláh has advocated is an international Supreme Tribunal to adjudicate on any sources of conflict and contention:

His third teaching is that religion is a mighty stronghold,

but that it must engender love, not malevolence and hate. Should it lead to malice, spite, and hate, it is of no value at all. For religion is a remedy, and if the remedy bring on disease, then put it aside. Again, as to religious, racial, national and political bias: all these prejudices strike at the very root of human life; one and all they beget bloodshed, and the ruination of the world. So long as these prejudices survive, there will be continuous and fearsome wars.

To remedy this condition there must be universal peace. To bring this about, a Supreme Tribunal must be established, representative of all governments and peoples; questions both national and international must be referred thereto, and all must carry out the decrees of this Tribunal. Should any government or people disobey, let the whole world arise against that government or people.[9]

The eventual aim of the Bahá'í Faith is the achievement of a world at peace and a world civilization.

A world community in which all economic barriers will have been permanently demolished and the interdependence of Capital and Labour definitely recognized; in which the clamour of religious fanaticism and strife will have been forever stilled; in which the flame of racial animosity will have been finally extinguished; in which a single code of international law – the product of the considered judgement of the world's federated representatives – shall have as its sanction the instant and coercive intervention of the combined forces of the federated units; and finally a world community in which the fury of a capricious and militant nationalism will have been transmuted into an abiding consciousness of world citizenship – such indeed, appears, in its broadest outline, the Order anticipated by Bahá'u'lláh, an Order that shall come to be regarded as the fairest fruit of a slowly maturing age.[10]

Most of the rest of the social teachings of Bahá'u'lláh can be seen as ways of bringing about the peace of the world and the unity of humankind. These teachings can be divided between those which deal with the undesirable tendencies that need to be eliminated from the world and those which concern the goals that need to be achieved to help the establishment of peace. Each of these goals needs to be worked for by the individual as well as on the national and international levels.

Eliminating the Disparity between the Rich and the Poor

World peace will never be established as long as the extremes of wealth and poverty exist. The huge inequality in the distribution of wealth is one of the most important causes of the present world instability and must be addressed by the governments of the world both individually and collectively.

> It is evident that under present systems and conditions of government the poor are subject to the greatest need and distress while others more fortunate live in luxury and plenty far beyond their actual necessities. This inequality of portion and privilege is one of the deep and vital problems of human society. That there is need of an equalization and apportionment by which all may possess the comforts and privileges of life is evident. There must be legislative readjustment of conditions. The rich too must be merciful to the poor, contributing from willing hearts to their needs without being forced or compelled to do so. The composure of the world will be assured by the establishment of this principle in the religious life of mankind.[11]

On the level of the individual, this becomes a spiritual principle:

> Bestow My wealth upon My poor, that in heaven thou mayest draw from stores of unfading splendour and treasures of imperishable glory.[12]

Tell the rich of the midnight sighing of the poor, lest heed-lessness lead them into the path of destruction, and deprive them of the Tree of Wealth. To give and to be generous are attributes of Mine; well is it with him that adorneth himself with My virtues.[13]

One of the key factors that maintains poverty in the world is the amount of money governments spend on armaments. Some of the poorest countries spend large amounts of their money buying weapons. Even the economies of the richer countries suffer as a result of this excessive expenditure on armaments. Over one hundred years ago 'Abdu'l-Bahá pointed out the folly of this:

> . . . night and day they are all straining every nerve to pile up more weapons of war, and to pay for this their wretched people must sacrifice most of whatever they are able to earn by their sweat and toil. How many thousands have given up work in useful industries and are labouring day and night to produce new and deadlier weapons which would spill out the blood of the race more copiously than before.[14]

The Bahá'í Faith teaches, however, that absolute equality, as advocated in communism, is both impossible to achieve and undesirable. Every individual has unique capacities and abilities and this means that there will always be differences in the wealth of individuals in a society. What Bahá'u'lláh advocates is the elimination of the extremes of wealth and poverty.

Eliminating Racism

Racism is a major barrier to peace. It is destructive of human dignity and destroys the unity of every society that it affects.

> Racism, one of the most baneful and persistent evils, is a major barrier to peace. Its practice perpetrates too outra-

geous a violation of the dignity of human beings to be countenanced under any pretext. Racism retards the unfoldment of the boundless potentialities of its victims, corrupts its perpetrators, and blights human progress. Recognition of the oneness of mankind, implemented by appropriate legal measures, must be universally upheld if this problem is to be overcome.[15]

Eliminating Unbridled Nationalism

While a limited degree of patriotism is healthy for a society, extreme nationalism that seeks to override the rights of other nations leads to conflict and makes peaceful co-existence impossible.

> That one indeed is a man who, today, dedicateth himself to the service of the entire human race. The Great Being saith: Blessed and happy is he that ariseth to promote the best interests of the peoples and kindreds of the earth. In another passage He hath proclaimed: It is not for him to pride himself who loveth his own country, but rather for him who loveth the whole world. The earth is but one country, and mankind its citizens.[16]

> Let there be no misgivings as to the animating purpose of the world-wide Law of Bahá'u'lláh. Far from aiming at the subversion of the existing foundations of society, it seeks to broaden its basis, to remould its institutions in a manner consonant with the needs of an ever-changing world . . . Its purpose is neither to stifle the flame of a sane and intelligent patriotism in men's hearts, nor to abolish the system of national autonomy so essential if the evils of excessive centralization are to be avoided. It does not ignore, nor does it attempt to suppress, the diversity of ethnic origins, of climate, of history, of language and tradition, of thought and habit, that differentiate the peoples

BUDDHISM AND THE BAHÁ'Í FAITH

and nations of the world. It calls for a wider loyalty, for a larger aspiration than any that has animated the human race.[17]

Eliminating Religious Strife

Religion has been a major source of conflict and wars in the history of the world. Bahá'u'lláh instructs the Bahá'ís:

'Consort with the followers of all religions in a spirit of friendliness and fellowship.' Whatsoever hath led the children of men to shun one another, and hath caused dissensions and divisions amongst them, hath, through the revelation of these words, been nullified and abolished.[18]

That the divers communions of the earth, and the manifold systems of religious belief, should never be allowed to foster the feelings of animosity among men, is, in this Day, of the essence of the Faith of God and His Religion. These principles and laws, these firmly established and mighty systems, have proceeded from one Source, and are the rays of one Light. That they differ one from another is to be attributed to the varying requirements of the ages in which they were promulgated.[19]

Promoting the Emancipation of Women

Women have a major role to play in establishing universal peace. If they can achieve a more equal position in society, their natural inclination towards peace will help create the conditions in which peace can be established.

Women and men have been and will always be equal . . .[20]

And among the teachings of Bahá'u'lláh is the equality of women and men. The world of humanity has two wings – one is women and the other men. Not until both wings are equally developed can the bird fly. Should one wing remain weak, flight is impossible. Not until the world of women becomes equal to the world of men in the acquisition of virtues and perfections, can success and prosperity be attained as they ought to be.[21]

. . . the principle of religion has been revealed by Bahá'u'lláh that woman must be given the privilege of equal education with man and full right to his prerogatives. That is to say, there must be no difference in the education of male and female in order that womankind may develop equal capacity and importance with man in the social and economic equation. Then the world will attain unity and harmony. In past ages humanity has been defective and inefficient because it has been incomplete. War and its ravages have blighted the world; the education of woman will be a mighty step toward its abolition and ending, for she will use her whole influence against war.[22]

Promoting Universal Education

Much of the strife and conflict in the world today is based on ignorance. This can be overcome through education. But this education must be a moral education as well as the instilling of facts.

Man is the supreme Talisman. Lack of a proper education hath, however, deprived him of that which he doth inherently possess . . . Regard man as a mine rich in gems of inestimable value. Education can, alone, cause it to reveal its treasures, and enable mankind to benefit therefrom. [23]

The primary, the most urgent requirement is the promotion of education. It is inconceivable that any nation should achieve prosperity and success unless this paramount, this fundamental concern is carried forward. The principal reason for the decline and fall of peoples is ignorance.[24]

Education in the Bahá'í teachings is used in its widest sense, meaning moral, spiritual and intellectual education. Bahá'ís believe that it is often through the lack of such education that humans experience difficulties and suffering arises, rather than through bad *Kamma*.

Promoting Communication among People

Strife and conflict often arise because of misunderstandings and poor communications.

> From the beginning of time the light of unity hath shed its divine radiance upon the world, and the greatest means for the promotion of that unity is for the peoples of the world to understand one another's writing and speech.[25]

Bahá'u'lláh advises the adoption of a universal language. Which language this is to be should be agreed upon by the nations.

> Each person will require training in two languages: his native tongue and the universal auxiliary form of speech. This will facilitate intercommunication and dispel the misunderstandings which the barriers of language have occasioned in the world.[26]

Other Bahá'í teachings include:

The Importance of Agriculture

Many of the poorer countries of the world, taking the industrial nations of the West as their example, have assumed that the best way to achieve an improvement in the standard of living of their people is to concentrate on developing their industry. The Bahá'í view, however, is that agriculture is the basis of any nation; therefore it must be given priority in the allocation of resources. In one of his works Bahá'u'lláh gives a list of several of his most important social teachings. After listing four of these, he writes:

Fifth: Special regard must be paid to agriculture. Although it hath been mentioned in fifth place, unquestionably it precedeth the others.[27]

In a statement to the World Food Council, the Bahá'í International Community wrote:

The inadequate level of food production in certain parts of the world, particularly in peasant agriculture in developing countries, should most fundamentally be countered by according higher social prestige to the agricultural sector and paying more attention to the needs and desires of peasant farmers. It should be noted that agriculture is in a sense the backbone and foundation of the economy and that this must be fully taken into account both in designing overall public policies and in implementing them.[28]

Great importance should be paid to rural areas. In the Bahá'í writings there are several suggestions for the organization of rural communities in ways that will improve their financial stability and self-sufficiency.

The Harmony of Religion and Science

Many people think of religion and science as being two opposing forces in human society. It is often considered that the advances of science inevitably mean that the influence of religion will diminish.

We may think of science as one wing and religion as the other; a bird needs two wings for flight, one alone would be useless. Any religion that contradicts science or that is opposed to it, is only ignorance — for ignorance is the opposite of knowledge. [29]

The Independent Investigation of Reality

In many of his writings Bahá'u'lláh has stressed the need

for every person to investigate the truth, particularly religious truth, for himself and not to rely on the words of others. For relying on the word of others leads to stagnation and decay in society, while independence of thought leads to progress and the welfare of humanity. The Buddha recognized this and in many places in the Buddhist scriptures he condemns those who blindly follow a teaching without investigating it for themselves. In one significant passage he advises:

> Now look you, Kalamas. Do not accept anything on [mere] hearsay (i.e. thinking that thus have we heard it from a long time). Do not accept anything by mere tradition (i.e. thinking that it has been handed down through many generations). Do not accept anything on account of mere rumours (i.e. by believing what others say without any investigation) . . . Do not accept anything merely because it agrees with your preconceived notions. Do not accept anything merely because it seems acceptable (i.e. thinking that as the speaker seems to be a good person his word should be accepted). Do not accept anything thinking that the ascetic is respected by us (therefore it is right to accept his word).
>
> But, Kalamas, if at any time you know for yourselves that something is spiritually unprofitable, blameworthy, conducive to loss and sorrow, then indeed, Kalamas, reject this. And if at any time you know for yourselves that something is spiritually profitable, is blameless, is conducive to gain and happiness, then, Kalamas, do you undertake that thing and abide therein.[30]

Similarly, Bahá'u'lláh writes of the qualities needed by the true seeker if he is to achieve the goal of attaining certitude:

> But, O my brother, when a true seeker determines to take the step of search in the path leading to the knowledge of the Ancient of Days, he must, before all else, cleanse and purify his heart . . . from the obscuring dust of all acquired

knowledge, and the allusions of the embodiments of satanic fancy. He must purge his breast . . . of every defilement, and sanctify his soul from all that pertaineth to water and clay, from shadowy and ephemeral attachments. He must so cleanse his heart that no remnant of either love or hate may linger therein, lest that love blindly incline him to error, or that hate repel him away from the truth . . . He must never seek to exalt himself above any one, must wash away from the tablet of his heart every trace of pride and vainglory, must cling unto patience and resignation, observe silence, and refrain from idle talk . . .

That seeker should also regard backbiting as grievous error . . . He should be content with little, and be free from all inordinate desire. He should treasure the companionship of those that have renounced the world, and regard avoidance of boastful and worldly people a precious benefit . . . He should not wish for others that which he doth not wish for himself, nor promise that which he doth not fulfil.

. . . When the detached wayfarer and sincere seeker hath fulfilled these essential conditions, then and only then can he be called a true seeker . . .

Only when the lamp of search, of earnest striving, of longing desire, of passionate devotion, of fervid love, of rapture, and ecstasy, is kindled within the seeker's heart . . . will the darkness of error be dispelled, the mists of doubts and misgivings be dissipated, and the lights of knowledge and certitude envelop his being.[31]

The Structure of the Universal Sangha – The Bahá'í Community

In the previous section the social teachings of Bahá'u'lláh were outlined. However, these are not merely ideas that Bahá'u'lláh has put forward and then left the Bahá'ís to carry out as best they can. He has also provided an outline of the social structures that will enable these principles to be put into practice. As we have discussed previously, the social structures that now exist are no longer adequate. They hold humanity back from progress and development. The present social structures reinforce those factors that divide society. They give strength to caste and race differences. They increase the gap between the poor and the rich. They often mean that only the most wealthy and influential have a say in the running of the affairs of the community.

Bahá'ís believe that Bahá'u'lláh has given humanity the plans for a new way of organizing society. This way is designed to lead to a society in which there will no longer be any extremes of poverty and wealth and in which all people will be more involved in the affairs of the community. Above all, Bahá'u'lláh's plans will lead to greater social justice. Bahá'ís around the world are at present trying to put these plans into effect within their Bahá'í communities.

The important point is that all people are now part of the universal *Sangha* established by Bahá'u'lláh. All have the responsibility of prayer, of reading the scripture and the other laws given by Bahá'u'lláh (see Chapter 6). Membership of the Bahá'í community in any area is open to all. It does not matter what a person's race, sex, caste or religious background is. The Bahá'í community of an area consists of all adults and young people over 15 years of age who have voluntarily stated their belief in Bahá'u'lláh. They are registered as Bahá'ís together with their children. In the Bahá'í Faith there are no castes. All Bahá'ís – men and women, young and old – are equal within the community. The only differences lie in that children under the age of 15 are not obliged to fulfil the personal laws (see Chapter 6) and that those under the age of 21 are not able to vote or to be voted for in elections.

Bahá'í Institutions

In the Bahá'í community there are no priests or leaders. No individual person has authority by virtue of his or her learning, sanctity or birth. The source of authority in each local Bahá'í community rests entirely with elected councils called Local Spiritual Assemblies. A Bahá'í election is carried out by secret ballot. There are no parties, candidates or electioneering. At the local level, all of the adult Bahá'ís of an area, male or female, are eligible to vote and to be voted for. The Local Spiritual Assembly consists of the nine persons who receive the highest number of votes.

Once a year Bahá'ís gather at area conventions to elect delegates to a National Convention at which a National Spiritual Assembly is elected. Once again the system of election involves no candidates, no parties and no electioneering. All of the adult Bahá'ís in the country are eligible to be elected.

The members of both the Local Spiritual Assembly and the National Spiritual Assembly are elected to serve for one year. Once every five years the members of all of the National Spiritual Assemblies in the world meet for an International Convention. At this they elect the Universal House of Justice, which is the highest authority in the Bahá'í world. All Bahá'ís accept the ultimate authority of the Universal House of Justice. The unity of the worldwide Bahá'í community is maintained by the presence of this single unifying authority, together with the Bahá'í scriptures, which consist of only that which exists in written authorized form.

It is these elected institutions that have authority in the Bahá'í Faith. No person, even if elected onto these institutions, has any individual authority.

In addition to the elected institutions there are a small number of individuals appointed to advise and encourage the Bahá'ís. The Counsellors and Auxiliary Board members and their assistants have no authority to direct or govern the Bahá'ís or their communities. At present they are appointed for terms of five years.

Bahá'u'lláh envisaged that these Bahá'í institutions would be the embryonic form of a future world order that would safeguard peace in the world.

Nineteen Day Feasts

The Bahá'í month consists of nineteen months of nineteen days. Once every Bahá'í month – in other words, every nineteen days – all the Bahá'ís in a particular Bahá'í community come together for the Nineteen Day Feast. The Feast consists of three parts: the first involves prayers, chants and other devotional activity; the second is administrative when the Local Spiritual Assembly reports to the community and the community consults and gives its suggestions to the Assembly; the third consists of the partaking of food and social activities.

Consultation

Whereas in the past decisions were made by individuals higher up the social scale or hierarchy and passed down without discussion, Bahá'u'lláh has introduced a new method of decision-making based on consultation. Everyone is involved in this process. The steps in the process of consultation are as follows:

- the Bahá'ís must gather in a spiritual atmosphere with a prayerful attitude

- the facts about the situation that requires a decision must be presented

- the spiritual principles involved in the situation must be found and discussed

- there must be a free and frank discussion of the

issue, taking care that all present their opinions and that no one dominates the proceedings

- a decision is arrived at preferably by consensus but otherwise by majority vote
- the decision is carried out by all in complete unity – in other words, with no regard to whether one voted for or against the decision

Bahá'ís believe that this process of consultation is able to tap the full resources of knowledge, wisdom and capabilities in the community. While it is a new and difficult skill to learn, it holds the key to the transformation of society.

Spiritual Guidance and Leadership

We have already noted above that there are no priests or religious leaders in the Bahá'í community. What then do Bahá'ís do when they have spiritual problems or need guidance? The Bahá'í teachings say that this age in which we are living is the age when humanity has reached its spiritual maturation. Therefore human beings should become more and more able to deal with these matters for themselves instead of needing to rely on others. There is help with this, however, in two ways. First, education for all is one of the social teachings of Bahá'u'lláh. All Bahá'ís should try hard to become literate so that they can read the scriptures for themselves. Through this, together with prayer and meditation, they can obtain divine guidance directly. Second, Bahá'ís are encouraged to bring any problems that they cannot deal with by themselves to their Local Spiritual Assembly. The method of consultation described above can be used not only for the administration of the community but also for spiritual guidance. In this way, each Bahá'í can draw on and use the collective wisdom of the group to help him or her.

The Bahá'í World Centre

The world centre of the Bahá'í Faith is in the Haifa-'Akká area to which Bahá'u'lláh was exiled by the Turkish Sultan. At that time it was part of the Turkish province of Syria; now it is part of the state of Israel. Haifa and 'Akká are two towns that face each other across a bay in the Mediterranean Sea. Together they form the spiritual and administrative centre of the Bahá'í Faith.

Near 'Akká is situated the Shrine of Bahá'u'lláh which is the spiritual centre of the Bahá'í world. Haifa is situated on Mount Carmel. Midway up Mount Carmel, at the centre of a series of monumental terraces, are the Shrines of the Báb and 'Abdu'l-Bahá. Next to these are the buildings of the world administrative centre of the Bahá'í Faith. Two of these, the Seat of the Universal House of Justice and the International Archives Building, have already been completed; work on three other buildings is in progress. From here the Universal House of Justice oversees the work of the worldwide Bahá'í community, corresponds with all of the National Spiritual Assemblies and sends messages to all of the Bahá'ís of the world. In turn, the National Spiritual Assemblies send reports of their activities and ask for guidance from the Universal House of Justice on difficult matters.

Through the work of the Bahá'í World Centre a global community is emerging and developing and people from all over the world are being linked together.

6

The *Vinaya*
Laws, Rituals and Festivals

While there is much similarly between the Bahá'í Faith and Buddhism, they do differ from one another in their practice. Every religion has its own laws, rituals and festivals. The Bahá'í Faith is an independent world religion. Therefore it does not seek to impose the laws and rituals of any previous religion on the whole world but rather has its own. In general, however, in comparison to other religions, the Bahá'í Faith has very little in the way of law and ritual.

The lack of personal laws, apart from the few mentioned below, means that the activities of Bahá'ís are guided more by moral principles than by laws. As has been mentioned previously, Bahá'u'lláh says that humanity has reached the age of maturity. This means we are leaving childhood and adolescence behind. This is the reason for the shift from specific laws to general moral principles: a mature adult humanity is expected to have learnt those codes of conduct which were taught it in previous ages by earlier Buddhas.

The comparative lack of ritual in the Bahá'í Faith means that major personal events, such as weddings, can be arranged by Bahá'ís as they wish incorporating, for example, elements of local tradition. This is permissible as long as these do not imply adherence to another religion.

Bahá'í Laws
Prayer, Reading the Scriptures and Meditation
Bahá'u'lláh says that all Bahá'ís must pray daily. To enable

them to fulfil this obligation, he has given them three prayers, one of which they must choose to say every day. One is very short and must be said between noon and sunset; a medium one must be said three times a day; and a long one is said once daily at any time. The following is the short prayer:

I bear witness, O my God, that Thou hast created me to know Thee and to worship Thee. I testify, at this moment, to my powerlessness and to Thy might, to my poverty and to Thy wealth.

There is none other God but Thee, the Help in Peril, the Self-Subsisting.[1]

There are many other prayers revealed by Bahá'u'lláh and 'Abdu'l-Bahá. These may be said at any time that a person feels a desire to pray.

All Bahá'ís should try to learn to read so that they can read the holy writings for themselves. Bahá'u'lláh has commanded the Bahá'ís to read a part of the holy writings every morning and evening. The aim of reading these passages should be to achieve a better and deeper understanding of them. Just as Gautama Buddha has said in the Dhammapada: 'Better than a thousand useless words is one single word that gives peace; better than a thousand useless verses is one single verse that gives peace,'[2] so Bahá'u'lláh also has written: 'Should a person recite but a single verse from the Holy Writings in a spirit of joy and radiance, this would be better for him than reciting all the Scriptures . . .'[3] If a person cannot read the writings then some of them can be committed to memory.

Both Buddhists and Bahá'ís believe in the power of the holy scripture when recited. Bahá'u'lláh writes:

Intone, O My servant, the verses of God that have been received by thee, as intoned by them who have drawn nigh unto Him, that the sweetness of thy melody may kindle thine own soul, and attract the hearts of all men. Whoso

reciteth, in the privacy of his chamber, the verses revealed
by God, the scattering angels of the Almighty shall scatter
abroad the fragrance of the words uttered by his mouth,
and shall cause the heart of every righteous man to throb.
Though he may, at first, remain unaware of its effect, yet
the virtue of the grace vouchsafed unto him must needs
sooner or later exercise its influence upon his soul.[4]

A person should read and say the prayers and readings in
the language he or she knows best. As the Bahá'í Faith has
spread all over the world, the Bahá'í writings have been
translated into over eight hundred languages.

When a Bahá'í wants something, he or she prays for it —
but the prayer must be for something that is appropriate:

God will answer the prayer of every servant if that prayer
is urgent. His mercy is vast, illimitable. He answers the
prayers of all His servants. He answers the prayer of this
plant. The plant prays potentially, 'O God! Send me rain!'
God answers the prayer, and the plant grows. God will
answer anyone . . .

But we ask for things which the divine wisdom does not
desire for us, and there is no answer to our prayer. His
wisdom does not sanction what we wish. We pray, 'O God!
Make me wealthy!' If this prayer were universally
answered, human affairs would be at a standstill. There
would be none left to work in the streets, none to till the
soil, none to build, none to run the trains. Therefore, it is
evident that it would not be well for us if all prayers were
answered. The affairs of the world would be interfered
with, energies crippled and progress hindered. But whatever we ask for which is in accord with divine wisdom, God
will answer. Assuredly!

For instance, a very feeble patient may ask the doctor to
give him food which would be positively dangerous to his
life and condition. He may beg for roast meat. The doctor
is kind and wise. He knows it would be dangerous to his
patient so he refuses to allow it. The doctor is merciful; the

patient, ignorant. Through the doctor's kindness the patient recovers; his life is saved. Yet the patient may cry out that the doctor is unkind, not good, because he refuses to answer his pleading.[5]

Prayer and the reading of the holy writings should be followed by a period of meditation:

Through the faculty of meditation man attains to eternal life; through it he receives the breath of the Holy Spirit – the bestowal of the Spirit is given in reflection and meditation.

The spirit of man is itself informed and strengthened during meditation; through it affairs of which man knew nothing are unfolded before his view. Through it he receives Divine inspiration, through it he receives heavenly food.

Meditation is the key for opening the doors of mysteries. In that state man abstracts himself: in that state man withdraws himself from all outside objects; in that subjective mood he is immersed in the ocean of spiritual life and can unfold the secrets of things-in-themselves. To illustrate this, think of man as endowed with two kinds of sight; when the power of insight is being used the outward power of vision does not see.[6]

Bahá'ís pray and meditate mostly in the privacy of their own homes. They do not use pictures or statues. This may seem hard to put into practice at first but is part of the spiritual maturing of humanity.

Fasting

All Bahá'ís should fast during the month preceding the New Year ('Alá, 2–20 March). Fasting for Bahá'ís means that no food and drink should be taken between sunrise and sunset. The following are excused from the fast: anyone who is ill or travelling more than nine hours (or two hours on foot); women who are pregnant or nursing; children under the age of 15 and people over 70.

Marriage Laws

The family is the basis of society and so marriage is given great importance in the Bahá'í teachings. Each man may only have one wife and each woman may have only one husband. Both the man and the woman must agree to the marriage. The parents of both partners must also agree so that the unity of the family is maintained. Bahá'í marriage is considered not only to be a physical union but also a spiritual one which will last through eternity.

Contraception is permitted if it is used to space out the birth of children in a marriage but not for preventing the birth of children altogether.

Sexual activity is allowed only within marriage.

Divorce is permitted in the unfortunate event that the marriage breaks down completely. However, it is strongly discouraged and every effort must be made to enable the couple to be reconciled. After separation, they must wait one full year before a divorce is granted.

Dietary Laws

Bahá'ís are permitted to eat any food. Vegetarian food has been recommended by 'Abdu'l-Bahá as being the most natural food for humankind. He indicates that, in the future, when the study of diet and nutrition is more advanced, all human beings will become vegetarians.[7] But Bahá'ís are free to be vegetarian or non-vegetarian.

Drugs, Alcohol and Tobacco

Bahá'ís are forbidden to take any of mind-altering or habit-forming drugs such as opium, heroin and marijuana (*bhang*). Alcohol is also a mind-altering and habit-forming drug and is forbidden. The smoking of tobacco is strongly discouraged as a filthy and unhealthy habit but it is not forbidden.

Death and Burial

All Bahá'ís should make a will so their wishes regarding their property may be known. In this will they should ask that they be buried according to Bahá'í law.

Bahá'í law states that the body should be buried within one hour's travelling distance of the place of death. Cremation is forbidden as it breaks the cycle of natural composition and decomposition.

A Bahá'í funeral is simple and dignified. A programme of prayers and passages from the holy books may be chosen. There is also a special prayer for burial which should be recited.

Involvement with Politics

Bahá'ís should not involve themselves in party and factional politics, nor even express a preference for a particular party. All such party political activity causes division and runs counter to the Bahá'í aim of uniting society.

Obedience to the Government and to the Law

Bahá'ís must obey the government of the country in which they live and must not break any of its laws. The only exception to this is if the government asks a Bahá'í to renounce the Bahá'í Faith. In that case a Bahá'í must refuse to comply. However, even then active opposition to the government is not permitted.

Gambling, Begging and Backbiting

Bahá'u'lláh forbids gambling and begging. Bahá'ís are

encouraged to earn their own living through a useful occupation such as a trade, craft, art or profession.

Talking about the faults of others is very strongly condemned. Bahá'u'lláh considers this one of the greatest of human faults as it harms all: the speaker, the hearer and the victim of such talk.

Other Matters

There are no Bahá'í laws that need to be followed in the matters of dress or the giving of names. There is only the advice of Bahá'u'lláh that a Bahá'í should be moderate in all such things.

The Bahá'í Calendar

The Bahá'í Faith has its own calendar beginning from AD 1844. The calendar uses solar years and consists of 19 months of 19 days each. The Bahá'í months are named after various spiritual qualities or divine attributes.

Bahá'í month	*Translation*	*Begins*
Bahá	Splendour	21 March
Jalál	Glory	9 April
Jamál	Beauty	28 April
'Aẓamat	Grandeur	17 May
Núr	Light	5 June
Raḥmat	Mercy	24 June
Kalimát	Words	13 July
Kamál	Perfection	1 August
Asmá'	Names	20 August
'Izzat	Might	8 September
Mashíyyat	Will	27 September
'Ilm	Knowledge	16 October
Qudrat	Power	4 November

Qawl	Speech	23 November
Masá'il	Questions	12 December
Sharaf	Honour	31 December
Sulṭán	Sovereignty	19 January
Mulk	Dominion	7 February
'Alá'	Loftiness	2 March

There are four additional days before the last month of the year ('Alá') which make the number of days up to 365. These are increased to five days in a leap year. These days are called the Ayyám-i-Há and are specially set aside for hospitality and the giving of presents.

Bahá'í Festivals

Bahá'í s celebrate festivals that commemorate particular sacred events. For historical information on these events, see Chapter 4.

Naw-Rúz (New year)	21 March
Riḍván – first day	21 April
Riḍván – ninth day	29 April
Riḍván – twelfth day	2 May
The Báb's declaration of his mission	23 May
Passing of Bahá'u'lláh	29 May
Martyrdom of the Báb	9 July
Birth of the Báb	20 October
Birth of Bahá'u'lláh	12 November

Bahá'í Houses of Worship

At present, Bahá'ís in most local communities have no special place of worship. They meet either in each other's homes or at a Bahá'í centre.

It is envisaged, however, that in the future in each town there will be built a house of worship (*Mashriqu'l-Adhkár*). This will become the spiritual centre of the community.

Around it will be built schools, libraries, medical facilities, orphanages and so on. At present Bahá'ís prefer to use their money on other projects and therefore only seven of these have been built around the world. The latest of these is a beautiful building in the shape of a lotus flower in New Delhi, India.

Bahá'í Shrines and Pilgrimages

The majority of the holy places of the Bahá'í world are at the Bahá'í world centre in the Haifa-'Akká area and in Iran and Iraq. These are places linked to the lives of the central figures of the religion. The shrines of the Báb, Bahá'u'lláh and 'Abdu'l-Bahá are all in the Haifa-'Akká area. Those Bahá'ís who can afford to do so without difficulty are encouraged to perform a pilgrimage to them. But the holy places in Iran and Iraq cannot at present be visited owing to persecutions of the Bahá'í Faith in those countries.

The Bahá'í Life

Bahá'u'lláh states that the new *Dhamma* that he brings is designed to completely revolutionize humanity's life on this planet. Through the ethical teachings (described in Chapter 1), the social teachings (described in Chapter 5), and the evolution of the Bahá'í administration into a new world order, the whole of humankind's individual and social life will be spiritualized and changed. This change must start with the individual, however. Each of us must live our lives according to the high standards inculcated in the Bahá'í writings (see Chapter 1).

Becoming a Bahá'í

There are no rituals involved in becoming a Bahá'í. What is required is that one's heart be touched by the spirit of the Bahá'í Faith; one must acknowledge Bahá'u'lláh's claim to be the Divine Teacher for this age; and one must be prepared to live by the laws that Bahá'u'lláh has given.

Living the Bahá'í Life

There are few rituals involved in being a Bahá'í. Rather it is part of humanity's growth to maturity that we are asked to take increasing responsibility for our own actions.

To be a Bahá'í means following the moral and ethical teachings of Bahá'u'lláh (see Chapter 1) and trying to put into effect his social teachings (see Chapter 5). The latter can best be implemented, however, by Bahá'ís acting collectively through the Bahá'í institutions. Every Bahá'í is urged to give his or her full support to this. The Bahá'í teachings exhort us to be of service to humanity. Indeed, being of service is the highest station of humanity. Work done in the spirit of service is equal to prayers and devotions.

Conclusion

The Bahá'í Faith is a world-encircling, universal religion. Bahá'ís are always loyal to the government in every country in which they live. Their main effort is directed towards building a peaceful society. Bahá'ís do not seek to undermine any person's religious faith. Because Bahá'ís believe that the source of all of the world's religions is one and the great founders of these religions are the appearance in the world of the same reality, Bahá'ís respect all religions. Lord Buddha is respected as just such a great teacher and everyone who becomes a Bahá'í thus must also come to believe in the Buddha. Thus the millions of Bahá'ís all around the world who would otherwise have never have believed in or respected the Buddha do so now because they are Bahá'ís.

The worldwide Bahá'í community offers those who join it a new family, in addition to their blood-relatives. Bahá'ís come from every culture and background but are united in working towards goals of peace and unity. In a world which has become increasingly complex and inter-related, where morality has decayed to an extreme degree, and where the religious and secular authorities are unable to solve the problems that face humanity or to give leadership and direction, the Bahá'í community offers the world a model of how it is possible for world peace to arise; it provides an impetus to renew the commitment of the individual to lead a pious and moral life in the circumstances of our modern world – to become in the words of Lord Buddha 'a stream-winner'.

Bibliography

'Abdu'l-Bahá. *Paris Talks*. Oakham: Bahá'í Publishing Trust, 1972.

—— *Selections from the Writings of 'Abdu'l-Bahá* (trans. by a Committee at the Bahá'í World Centre and by Marzieh Gail). Haifa: Bahá'í World Centre, 1978.

—— *The Promulgation of Universal Peace*. Wilmette, Ill.: Bahá'í Publishing Trust, 1982.

—— *The Secret of Divine Civilization*. Wilmette, Ill.: Bahá'í Publishing Trust, 1990.

—— *Some Answered Questions* (comp. and trans. Laura Clifford Barney). Wilmette, Ill.: Bahá'í Publishing Trust, 1981.

Bahá'í International Community statement to Eleventh Ministerial Session of the World Food Council, Paris, France, 10–13 June 1985.

Bahai Scriptures (ed. Horace Holley). New York: Bretano's, 1923.

Bahá'í World Faith. Wilmette, Ill.: Bahá'í Publishing Trust, 2nd edn. 1976.

Bahá'u'lláh. *Book of Certitude (Kitáb-i-Íqán)* (trans. Shoghi Effendi). London: Bahá'í Publishing Trust, 3rd ed., 1982.

—— *Epistle to the Son of the Wolf* (trans. Shoghi Effendi). Wilmette, Ill.: Bahá'í Publishing Trust, 1988.

—— *Gleanings from the Writings of Bahá'u'lláh* (trans. Shoghi Effendi). London: Bahá'í Publishing Trust, rev. edn. 1978.

—— *The Hidden Words*. Wilmette, Ill.: Bahá'í Publishing Trust, 1990.

—— *Prayers and Meditations by Bahá'u'lláh*. London: Bahá'í Publishing Trust, 1978.

—— *The Seven Valleys and the Four Valleys* (trans. Marzieh Gail). Wilmette, Ill.: Bahá'í Publishing Trust, 1991.

—— *Tablets of Bahá'u'lláh Revealed after the Kitáb-i-Aqdas* (trans. Habib Taherzadeh). Haifa: Bahá'í World Centre, 1978.

Book of Discipline (trans. I.B. Horner) Sacred Books of the Buddhists, vols. 10–11, 13–14, 20, 25, 1938–66.

Buddhism in Translation (trans. Henry C. Warren). Harvard Oriental Series, vol. 3. Cambridge, Mass.: Harvard University, 1896.

Buddhist Scriptures (trans. Edward Conze). Harmondsworth: Penguin, 1959.

Buddhist Suttas (trans. T.W. Rhys Davids). Sacred Books of the East, vol. 11. Oxford: Clarendon Press, 1881.

Buddhist Texts: Through the Ages (ed. Edward Conze). Oxford: Bruno Cassirer, 1954.

Chauhan (Villiers-Stuart), Katherine. 'The Bahá'í Message – Any Concern of Buddhists?' Unpublished manuscript.

Dhammapada, The (trans. Juan Mascaro). Harmondsworth: Penguin, 1973.

Dialogues of the Buddha (trans. T.W. and C.A.F. Rhys Davids). Sacred Books of the Buddhists, vols. 2–4. London: Henry Frowde (vols. 1 and 2) and Humphrey Milford (vol. 3), 1899–1921.

Divine Art of the Living, The (comp. Mabel Hyde Paine). Wilmette, Ill.: Bahá'í Publishing Trust, 1986.

Esslemont, John E. *Bahá'u'lláh and the New Era*. London: Bahá'í Publishing Trust, 4th rev. edn. 1976.

Fozdar, Jamshed K. *Buddha Maitrya-Amitabha Has Appeared*. New Delhi: Bahá'í Publishing Trust, 1976.

Further Dialogues of the Buddha. (trans. Lord Chalmers). Sacred Books of the Buddhists, vols. 5–6. London: Humphrey Milford, 1926–7.

Gradual Sayings of the Buddha. Vols. 1–2, trans. F.L. Woodward, 1932–33; vols. 3–4, trans. E.M. Hart, 1934–5; vol. 5, trans. F.L. Woodward, 1936. London: Pali Text Society.

Importance of Prayer, Meditation and the Devotional Attitude, The. A compilation of the Universal House of Justice. Oakham, England: Bahá'í Publishing Trust, 1981.

Kindred Sayings, Book of. Vols. 1–2 trans. C.A.F. Rhys Davids; vols. 3–5 trans. F.L. Woodward). London: Pali Text Society, 1922?–30.

Masefield, Peter. 'The Muni and the Moonies', *Religion*, vol. 15, 1985, pp. 143–60.

Middle Length Sayings, The Collection of (trans. I.B. Horner). 3 vols. London: Luzacs for Pali Text Society, 1954–9.

Minor Anthologies of the Pali Canon. Vols. 7–9, pt 1 *Dhammapada*, trans. C.A.F. Rhys Davids, 1931; pt 2 *Udana*, trans. F.L. Woodward, 1935. Sacred Books of the Buddhists. London; Humphrey Milfold.

Momen, Moojan. *Hinduism and the Bahá'í Faith.* Oxford: George Ronald, 1990.

—— 'Relativism as the Basis of Bahá'í Metaphysics.' *Studies in Honor of the Late Hasan M. Balyuzi* (ed. M. Momen). Los Angeles: Kalimat Press, 1988, pp. 185–217.

Murti, T.R.V. *The Central Philosophy of Buddhism*, London: Mandala, 1980.

Parry, Robert. 'Faith – Buddhism and Bahá'í, with special emphasis on Theravada.' Unpublished manuscript, 1993.

Shoghi Effendi. *God Passes By*. Wilmette, Ill.: Bahá'í Publishing Trust, 1979.

—— *The World Order of Bahá'u'lláh*. Wilmette, Ill.: Bahá'í Publishing Trust, 1980.

The Universal House of Justice. *The Promise of World Peace*. Various editions. 1985.

Vinaya Texts (trans. T.W. Rhys Davids & H. Oldenberg).

Sacred Books of the East, vol. 20. Oxford: Clarendon Press, 1885.

Women. A compilation of the Universal House of Justice. London: Bahá'í Publishing Trust, 1986.

Woven Cadences (trans. E.M. Hare). Sacred Books of the Buddhists, vol. 15, c. 1945.

References

1. The Path – The *Dhamma*

1. *Majjhima Nikaya*, 1:428, v. 34–429, v. 28; sutta 63; translated in Warren, *Buddhism in Translation*, p. 120.
2. Bahá'u'lláh, *Book of Certitude*, p. 49.
3. Bahá'u'lláh, *Gleanings*, no. CVI, p. 212.
4. *Digha Nikaya* 2:305–7; cf translation in *Buddhist Scriptures*, p. 186 and *Dialogues of the Buddha*, vol. 2, pp. 337–9.
5. 'Abdu'l-Bahá, *Selections*, p. 200.
6. ibid. pp. 220–1.
7. *Digha Nikaya* 2:308–10; cf translation in *Buddhist Scriptures*, p. 186 and *Dialogues of the Buddha*, vol. 2, pp. 339–41.
8. 'Abdu'l-Bahá, *Paris Talks*, p. 110.
9. Bahá'u'lláh, *Gleanings*, no. CLIII, pp. 325–6.
10. *Digha Nikaya* 2:310–11; cf translation in *Buddhist Scriptures*, p. 187 and *Dialogues of the Buddha*, vol. 2, pp. 341–3.
11. *Dhammapada* 336.
12. Bahá'u'lláh, *Gleanings*, no. LXXI, p. 137.
13. Bahá'u'lláh, *Hidden Words*, Persian no. 40.
14. Bahá'u'lláh, *Gleanings*, no. CXXVIII, pp. 274–5.
15. Bahá'u'lláh, *Tablets*, p. 69.
16. *Dhammapada* 146.
17. *Dhammapada* 235.

18. Bahá'u'lláh, *Hidden Words*, Persian no. 20.
19. ibid. no. 21.
20. *Digha Nikaya* (2:312) 22, Maha Satipatthana Sutta:21; translated in *Dialogues of the Buddha*, vol. 2, p. 343.
21. Bahá'u'lláh, *Tablets*, p. 157.
22. 'Abdu'l-Bahá, in *Divine Art of Living*, p. 66.
23. *Digha Nikaya* (2:312) 22, Maha Satipatthana Sutta:21; translated in *Dialogues of the Buddha*, vol. 2, pp. 343–4.
24. 'Abdu'l-Bahá, *Secret of Divine Civilization*, p. 98.
25. *Digha Nikaya* (2:312) 22, Maha Satipatthana Sutta:21; translated in *Dialogues of the Buddha*, vol. 2, p. 344.
26. *Dhammapada* 354.
27. *Dhammapada* 133.
28. *Dhammapada* 176.
29. Bahá'u'lláh, *Book of Certitude*, pp. 123–4.
30. 'Abdu'l-Bahá, in *Bahá'í World Faith*, p. 384.
31. *Digha Nikaya* (2:312) 22, Maha Satipatthana Sutta:21; translated in *Dialogues of the Buddha*, vol. 2, p. 344.
32. Bahá'u'lláh, *Gleanings*, no. CXXXIX, p. 305.
33. *Dhammapada* 295, 314, 51.
34. Bahá'u'lláh, *Hidden Words*, Persian no. 76.
35. Bahá'u'lláh, *Tablets*, p. 156.
36. *Digha Nikaya* (2:312) 22, Maha Satipatthana Sutta:21; translated in *Dialogues of the Buddha*, vol. 2, p. 344.
37. Bahá'u'lláh, *Hidden Words*, Persian no. 82.
38. Bahá'u'lláh, *Tablets*, p. 26.
39. *Digha Nikaya* (2:312) 22, Maha Satipatthana Sutta:21; translated in *Dialogues of the Buddha*, vol. 2, p. 344.
40. Bahá'u'lláh, *Gleanings*, no. XXXIV, p. 81.
41. ibid. no. CLI, p. 320.
42. 'Abdu'l-Bahá, *Paris Talks,* p. 87.
43. *Digha Nikaya* (2:312) 22, Maha Satipatthana Sutta:21; translated in *Dialogues of the Buddha*, vol. 2, pp. 344–5.

44. Bahá'u'lláh, *Gleanings*, no. LX, pp. 117–8.
45. Bahá'u'lláh, *Hidden Words*, Persian no. 44.
46. *Digha Nikaya* (2:312) 22, Maha Satipatthana Sutta:21; translated in *Dialogues of the Buddha*, vol. 2, p. 345.
47. 'Abdu'l-Bahá, *Paris Talks*, pp. 174–6.
48. *Dhammapada* 47.
49. Bahá'u'lláh, *Hidden Words*, Persian no. 75.
50. *Dhammapada* 50, 252.
51. Bahá'u'lláh, *Hidden Words*, Arabic nos. 26, 27; Persian nos. 66, 44.
52. *Dhammapada* 78.
53. Bahá'u'lláh, *Hidden Words*, Persian no. 56.
54. *Dhammapada* 405.
55. 'Abdu'l-Bahá, *Selections*, no. 138, p. 160.
56. *Dhammapada* 197, 200.
57. 'Abdu'l-Bahá, *Paris Talks*, p. 109.
58. *Dhammapada* 204.
59. 'Abdu'l-Bahá, in *Bahá'í World Faith*, p. 375.
60. *Dhammapada* 129, 131, 132, 137.
61. 'Abdu'l-Bahá, *Selections*, no. 8, p. 24.
62. *Dhammapada* 184.
63. Bahá'u'lláh, *Gleanings*, no. V, p. 8.
64. *Dhammapada* 2.
65. Bahá'u'lláh, *Gleanings*, no. CXLI, p. 306.
66. *Dhammapada* 5.
67. Bahá'u'lláh, in *Bahá'í Scriptures*, p. 249.
68. 'Abdu'l-Bahá, *Paris Talks*, p. 179.
69. *Dhammapada* 177.
70. Bahá'u'lláh, *Hidden Words*, Persian no. 49.
71. *Dhammapada* 221, 223.
72. 'Abdu'l-Bahá, *Selections*, no. 9, p. 26.
73. 'Abdu'l-Bahá, *Paris Talks*, p. 29.
74. *Digha Nikaya*, 2:80, Maha-Parinibbana Sutta 1:11; translated in *Buddhist Suttas*, p. 10.

75. Bahá'u'lláh, *Gleanings*, no. CXXX, p. 284.

2. The Structure of Existence

1. *Majjhima Nikaya* (1:426) 2:2:63, Culla Malunkya Sutta, v. 43; translated in *Middle Length Sayings*, vol. 2, p. 99 and Warren, *Buddhism in Translation*, p. 120.
2. ibid.
3. Bahá'u'lláh, *Tablets*, p. 140.
4. Bahá'u'lláh, *Gleanings*, no. LXXXII, pp. 161–2.
5. ibid. p. 158.
6. ibid. no. LXXXIII, pp. 164–5. See also ibid. no. I, pp. 3–5. cf no. XIX, pp. 46–7.
7. ibid. no. XXVI, p. 62.
8. See Momen 'Relativism', in Momen, *Balyuzi*, pp. 185–217.
9. *Digha Nikaya*, Maha-Sudassana Sutta, 2:42; translated in *Buddhist Suttas*, p. 289.
10. Bahá'u'lláh, *Prayers and Meditations*, no. LXX, p. 116.
11. Bahá'u'lláh, *Tablets*, p. 219.
12. *Dhammapada* 170.
13. Bahá'u'lláh, *Gleanings*, no. CLIII, p. 327.
14. 'Abdu'l-Bahá, *Selections*, no. 150, p. 177–8.
15. *Digha Nikaya*, Maha-Sudassana Sutta, 2:39; translated in *Buddhist Suttas*, p. 288.
16. Bahá'u'lláh, *Hidden Words*, Persian no. 14.
17. *Udana* 8:3; cf translation in *Minor Anthologies*, p. 98. Nagarjuna, the founder of the Madhyamika school of Buddhism, argues from this passage that without the acceptance of an Ultimate Reality (*Paramartha*) there can be no deliverance (*Nirvana*). *Madhyamika Karikas*, ed. L. de la Vallée Poussin (Bib. Buddh. 4) XXIV, 10, see Murti, p. 235.
18. Bahá'u'lláh, *Book of Certitude*, pp. 63–4.
19. Bahá'u'lláh, *Gleanings*, no. LXXXI, p. 157.
20. ibid.
21. Bahá'u'lláh, *Prayers and Meditations*, p. 91.

22. Bahá'u'lláh, *Book of Certitude*, p. 115.
23. Bahá'u'lláh, *Seven Valleys*, p. 36.
24. Bahá'u'lláh, *Gleanings*, no. CXXXVI, p. 293.
25. ibid. no. XLIII, p. 93.
26. *Jataka* 3:370–3, no. 407; translated in *Buddhist Texts*, p. 85
27. 'Abdu'l-Bahá, *Paris Talks*, pp. 49–50.
28. ibid. pp. 50–1.
29. 'Abdu'l-Bahá, *Selections*, p. 185.
30. *Sutta Nipata* 1076, *Parayana Vagga* 5:6; cf translation in Hare, *Woven Cadences*, p. 155.
31. Bahá'u'lláh, *Gleanings*, no. LXXXI, p. 155.
32. *Udana* 8, 1; cf translation in Woodward, *Minor Anthologies* p. 97.
33. *Dhammapada* 180–1.
34. *Dhammapada* 92–4.
35. *Samyutta Nikaya* 3:83–4; cf translation in *Kindred Sayings* vol. 3, p. 69.
36. *Dhammapada* 87–9.
37. Bahá'u'lláh, *Gleanings*, no. LXXII, p. 139.
38. ibid. no. CXV, p. 240.
39. Bahá'u'lláh, *Hidden Words*, Persian no. 55.
40. Bahá'u'lláh, *Gleanings* no. LXXXI, p. 156.
41. Bahá'u'lláh, *Hidden Words*, Persian no. 70.
42. 'Abdu'l-Bahá, *Paris Talks*, p. 110.
43. *Samyutta Nikaya* (4:400) part 10:44, *Avyakata Samyut tam*:10; translated in *Book of Kindred Sayings*, vol. 4, p. 282
44. *Majjhima Nikaya* 2:3:72, *Aggi-Vacchagotta Sutta*; quoted in Murti, *Central Philosophy of Buddhism*, p. 44; see also translation in Warren, *Buddhism in Translation*, p. 124– and *Middle Length Sayings*, vol. 2, pp. 97–101.
45. *Samyutta Nikaya*, vol. 3, p. 118; cf translation in *Buddhist Texts*, p. 106.
46. *Digha Nikaya*, Tevigga Sutta, 1, 42, 43; translated in *Buddhist Suttas*, pp. 185–6.

47. *Digha Nikaya:* 13, Tevigga Sutta 1:42–3; translated in *Buddhist Suttas,* p. 186.
48. *Majjhima Nikaya* 1:71; cf translation in Horner, *Middle Length Sayings,* 1:95–6.
49. *Digha Nikaya,* Tevigga Sutta, 1, 44; translated in *Buddhist Suttas,* pp. 186–7 and *Dialogues of the Buddha,* vol. 1, pp. 316–17.
50. *Samyutta Nikaya,* 5:442; cf translation in *Kindred Sayings,* vol. 5, p. 374.
51. Bahá'u'lláh, *Gleanings,* no. XIX, pp. 46–7.
52. *Digha Nikaya* (2:154) 16, Maha-Parinibbana Sutta 6:6; translated in *Dialogues of the Buddha,* vol. 2, p. 173.
53. *Digha Nikaya* (2:148) 16, Maha-Parinibbana Sutta 5:24; translated in *Dialogues of the Buddha* vol. 2, p. 164; a similar statement occurs in *Dhammapada* 182.
54. *Dhammapada* 272.
55. *Samyutta Nikaya,* 3:118; translated in *Buddhist Texts,* p. 106.
56. *Digha Nikaya,* Tevigga Sutta 43; translated in *Buddhist Suttas,* p. 186 or *Dialogues of the Buddha,* vol. 1, p. 315.
57. *Majjhima Nikaya* 3, Ganaka-Moggalana Sutta:107; translated in *Further Dialogues of the Buddha,* p. 158; and *Middle Length Sayings,* vol. 3, p. 56.
58. *Samyutta Nikaya* (3:60), chap. 22:58; translated in *Kindred Sayings* vol. 3, p. 58.
59. *Dhammapada* 255.
60. Bahá'u'lláh, *Seven Valleys,* p. 37. Bahá'u'lláh is here quoting from the Qur'án.
61. *Samyutta Nikaya* 3:120.
62. Bahá'u'lláh, *Gleanings,* no. XLIX, p. 102.
63. *Samyutta Nikaya* 5:442; translated in *Kindred Sayings,* vol. 5, p. 374.
64. *Samyutta Nikaya* (3:60), chap. 22:58; translated in *Kindred Sayings,* vol. 3, p. 58.

65. *Samyutta Nikaya* 2:104; cf translation in *Kindred Sayings*, vol. 2, p. 74.
66. Bahá'u'lláh, *Gleanings*, no. LXX, p. 136.
67. Bahá'u'lláh, *Hidden Words*, Introduction.
68. *Digha Nikaya*, 3:75–6; translated in *Dialogues of the Buddha*, vol. 3, pp. 73–4.
69. *Milandapanha*, p. 285; translated in *Buddhist Texts*, pp. 110–11.
70. Bahá'u'lláh, *Gleanings*, no. XXIV, p. 59.
71. Bahá'u'lláh, *Book of Certitude*, p. 113.
72. *Samyutta Nikaya* 5:437; translated in *Kindred Sayings*, vol. 5, p. 370.
73. 'Abdu'l-Bahá, *Bahá'í World Faith*, p. 383.
74. Bahá'u'lláh, *Gleanings*, no. LXXXVI, p. 169.
75. *Majjhima Nikaya* 1:123, 161, 193, 200; translated in *Middle Length Sayings*, vol. 1, 160, 205, 239, 247. *Samyutta Nikaya* 1:120; translated in *Kindred Sayings*, vol.1, p. 149. *Udana* 2:2; 3:8; translated in *Minor Anthologies*, vol. 2, p. 14, 37. *Sutta Nipata* 337, 2:11; translated in *Woven Cadences*, p. 50.
76. *Majjhima Nikaya* 1:179, 276, 344; translated in Horner, *Middle Length Sayings*, vol. 1, pp. 224, 333; vol. 2, p. 8.
77. See, for example, *Majjhima Nikaya*, 3:33, translated in Horner, *Middle Length Sayings*, 3:85.
78. *Anguttara Nikaya* 3:198; 4:359; 5:337; translated in *Gradual Sayings*, vol. 3, pp. 146–7.
79. *Sutta Nipata* 1:77, translated in Hare, *Woven Cadences*, p. 12. *Samyutta Nikaya* 1:171; translated in *Kindred Sayings*, vol. 1, p. 217.
80. *Samyutta Nikaya* 5:219; translated in *Kindred Sayings*, vol. 5, p. 194.
81. *Vinaya Pitaka*, Mahāvagga 6:247; translated in *Book of Discipline*, vol. 4, pp. 340–2.
82. See, for example, Bahá'u'lláh, *Book of Certitude*, p. 151, and 'Abdu'l-Bahá, *Some Answered Questions*, p. 130.

33. *Majjhima Nikaya*, 2:170; translated in *Middle Length Sayings*, vol. 2, pp. 360–1.

34. *Samyutta Nikaya* 1:36; translated in *Kindred Sayings*, vol. I, p. 51. *Majjhima Nikaya* 1:320, translated in Horner, *Middle Length Sayings*, 1:382.

35. 'Abdu'l-Bahá, *Bahá'í World Faith*, p. 364.

36. *Sutta Nipata* 1146; translated in *Woven Cadences*, pp. 166–7, and *Buddhist Texts*, p. 52; cf also 'By Faith the flood is crossed', *Sutta Nipata* 184; translated in *Buddhist Texts*, p. 54. In a commentary on this verse, in the *Milandapanha*, it is explained that faith takes a person into the stream aspiring to cross to the other side and thus become a stream-winner (*Milandapanha* 35–6; translated in *Buddhist Texts*, p. 54).

37. Bahá'u'lláh, *Book of Certitude*, pp. 73–4.

3. Prophecies of the Buddha

1. The Buddha's address in *Digha Nikaya* (3:75–6) Cakkavatti-Sihanada Suttana; translated in *Dialogues of the Buddha*, vol. 3, pp. 73–4.

2. The Buddha's address in *Digha Nikaya* (3:76) Cakkavatti-Sihanada Suttana; translated in *Dialogues of the Buddha*, vol. 3, p. 74.

3. *Anagatavamsa*, adapted from translation in *Buddhism in Translation*, pp. 481ff and *Buddhist Texts*, pp. 47–50.

4. See Fozdar, *Buddha Maitrya-Amitabha has Appeared*, pp. 213–85 for details of these calculations.

5. *Vinaya Pitaka* (2:253), Kullavaga 10:1:6; translated in *Vinaya Texts*, part 3, pp. 325–6.

6. Further examples showing that the dates associated with the life of Bahá'u'lláh are in agreement with Buddhist and Hindu prophecy are outlined in Fozdar, *Buddha Maitrya-Amitabha has Appeared*, pp. 213–85.

7. *Anagatavamsa*, cf translations in *Buddhism in Translation*, pp. 482ff and *Buddhist Texts*, pp. 47–50.
8. The Buddha's address in *Digha Nikaya* (3:70–2) Cakkavatti-Sihanada Suttana; translated in *Dialogues of the Buddha*, vol. 3, pp. 69–71.
9. *Samyutta Nikaya* (2:224) 16, Kassapa:13; translated in *Buddhist Texts*, p. 46 and *Kindred Sayings*, vol. 2, p. 152.
10. 'Abdu'l-Bahá, *Selections*, pp. 103–4.

4. The Life of Bahá'u'lláh

1. Bahá'u'lláh, *Epistle*, p. 22.
2. Avagosha, *Buddhacarita*; translated in *Buddhist Scripture* p. 52. A similar passage occurs in *Majjhima Nikaya* 1:167 v. 31–2; translated in *Buddhism in Translation*, p. 339.
3. Bahá'u'lláh, *Book of Certitude*, p. 251.
4. Bahá'u'lláh, quoted in Shoghi Effendi, *God Passes By*, p. 126.
5. *Digha Nikaya* 13, Tevigga Sutta:10–36; translated in *Dialogues of the Buddha*, vol. 1, pp. 303–14.
6. See *Digha Nikaya* 1:104ff, *Sutta Nipata* 284–306, *Anguttara Nikaya* 3:221ff, *Samyutta Nikaya* 4:117ff; quoted in Masefield, pp. 151–4.
7. Bahá'u'lláh, *Book of Certitude*, pp. 105–6.

5. The *Sangha*

1. *Digha Nikaya* 2:124–6; translated in *Dialogues of the Buddha*, vol. 2, pp. 133–6.
2. Bahá'u'lláh, *Hidden Words*, concluding words.
3. Maha-Parinibbana Sutta 1:6; translated in *Buddhist Suttas* pp. 6–7.
4. 'Abdu'l-Bahá, *Selections*, pp. 31–2.
5. Bahá'u'lláh, *Gleanings*, no. CXXI, p. 285.
6. ibid. no. CXXXII, p. 287.
7. ibid. no. CXVII, p. 248.
8. ibid. no. CXI, p. 216.

9. 'Abdu'l-Bahá, *Selections*, pp. 248–9.
10. Shoghi Effendi, *World Order*, p. 41.
11. 'Abdu'l-Bahá, *Promulgation*, p. 107.
12. Bahá'u'lláh, *Hidden Words*, Arabic no. 57.
13. ibid. Persian no. 49.
14. 'Abdu'l-Bahá, *Secret of Divine Civilization*, p. 61.
15. The Universal House of Justice, *Promise of World Peace*, para. 29.
16. Bahá'u'lláh, *Tablets*, p. 167.
17. Shoghi Effendi, *World Order*, pp. 41–2.
18. Bahá'u'lláh, *Gleanings*, no. XLIII, p. 94.
19. ibid. no. CXXXII, pp. 286
20. Bahá'u'lláh, quoted in *Women*, p. 23.
21. 'Abdu'l-Bahá, *Selections*, p. 302.
22. 'Abdu'l-Bahá, *Promulgation*, p. 108.
23. Bahá'u'lláh, *Tablets*, pp. 161–2.
24. 'Abdu'l-Bahá, *Secret of Divine Civilization*, p. 109.
25. Bahá'u'lláh, *Tablets*, p. 127.
26. 'Abdu'l-Bahá, *Promulgation*, p. 300.
27. Bahá'u'lláh, *Tablets*, p. 90.
28. Bahá'í International Community statement to Eleventh Ministerial Session of the World Food Council, Paris, France, 10–13 June 1985, p. 2.
29. 'Abdu'l-Bahá, *Paris Talks*, pp. 130–1.
30. *Anguttara Nikaya* 1:188; cf translation in *Gradual Sayings*, vol. 1, pp. 171–2.
31. Bahá'u'lláh, *Book of Certitude*, pp. 123–5.

6. The *Vinaya*

1. Bahá'u'lláh, *Prayers and Meditations*, no. 181, p. 240.
2. *Dhammapada* 100–1
3. Bahá'u'lláh, quoted in *Importance of Prayer, Meditation and the Devotional Attitude*, p. 3.
4. Bahá'u'lláh, *Gleanings*, no. CXXXVI, p. 294.

5. 'Abdu'l-Bahá, *Promulgation*, pp. 246–7.
6. 'Abdu'l-Bahá, *Paris Talks*, p. 175.
7. See Esslemont, *Bahá'u'lláh and the New Era*, p. 98.

Index

'Abdu'l-Bahá, 60, 66, 70, 87
  Shrine of, 82, 91
Absolute, the; Absolute
  Reality, vii, 17, 19–20,
  23–4, 28, 34, 38
  see also God
Administrative Order,
  Bahá'í, 60, 78–9
Agriculture, 74–5
Akaravati saddha, 45
'Akká, 59, 82, 91
Alcohol, 87–8
Amida Buddha, 43
Amulika saddha, 45
Ananda, 22, 32, 57
Anatta, 20, 25, 26
Anger, 14
Anicca, 20, 21
Animals
  kindness to, 12
  sacrifice of, 42
Armaments, 70
Asceticism, 4
Attachment, to material
  world, 2–4, 25, 30, 76
Auxiliary Board members,
  79

Avatars, 41, 54
Avyakatas (indeterminables),
  17–18, 24, 31–3
Ayyám–i–Há, 90

Báb, the, 55, 56, 90
  Shrine of, 82, 91
Bábí movement, 55
Backbiting, 7, 77, 88–9
Baghdad, 56
Bahá'í Faith, vi–vii, 48, 55,
  60, 68, 83, 92
Bahá'í International
  Community, 61, 74–5
Bahá'í life, 91–2
Bahá'í World Centre, 82
Bahá'ís, vi
  becoming a Bahá'í, 91–2
  community of, viii, 60–1, 64,
  77–82, 92–3
Bahá'u'lláh, vi, vii, 27, 47, 65,
  92
  life of, viii, 54–61, 81–2, 90
  mission of, 42, 65
  Shrine of, 82, 91
  teachings of, see Teachings,
  Bahá'í
Begging, 88–9

INDEX